LONGING FOR SPIRITUAL INTIMACY

THE

HEART

JEAN FLEMING

NAVPRESS

BRINGING TRUTH TO LIFE
NavPress Publishing Group
P.O. Box 35001, Colorado Springs, Colorado 80935

The Navigators is an international Christian organization. Jesus Christ gave His followers the Great Commission to go and make disciples (Matthew 28:19). The aim of The Navigators is to help fulfill that commission by multiplying laborers for Christ in every nation.

NavPress is the publishing ministry of The Navigators. NavPress publications are tools to help Christians grow. Although publications alone cannot make disciples or change lives, they can help believers learn biblical discipleship, and apply what they learn to their lives and ministries.

Library of Congress Catalog Card Number: 95-7297
ISBN 08910-99034

Cover photograph: Wood River Gallery

Some of the anecdotal illustrations in this book are true to life and are included with the permission of the persons involved. All other illustrations are composites of real situations, and any resemblance to people living or dead is coincidental.

Unless otherwise identified, all Scripture quotations in this publication are taken from the *HOLY BIBLE: NEW INTERNATIONAL VERSION*® (NIV®). Copyright © 1973, 1978, 1984 by International Bible Society. Used by permission of Zondervan Publishing House. All rights reserved. Other versions used include: the *Williams New Testament* (WMS) by Charles B. Williams, Copyright 1937, 1965, 1966, by Edith S. Williams, Moody Bible Institute of Chicago; and the *King James Version* (KJV).

Fleming, Jean
    The homesick heart : longing for spiritual intimacy / Jean Fleming.
        p. cm.
    ISBN 0-89109-903-4
    1. Desire for God. 2. Beatific vision. 3. Heaven—Christianity. 4. Spiritual life—Christianity. I. Title.
    BV4817.F57 1995
    233—dc20
                                                                    95-7297
                                                                    CIP

Printed in the United States of America

1 2 3 4 5 6 7 8 9 10 11 12 13 14 15 / 99 98 97 96 95

CONTENTS

To our longing God

INTRODUCTION

B ooks fall into categories. There are the "And then what happened?" books that have a story line. There are the "So what?" books that deal with facts, ideas, and information. And there are the "What's in it for me?" books that fall roughly within the self-help camp. But there's another category—the "Aha!" category. This is the kind of book I've written.

"Aha!" books are my favorite. They pull back a curtain to show me something that was there all along, something that registers as truth when I encounter it. Often I get the sense that the author was as surprised at the "showing" as I was. "Aha!" books don't try to prove anything. All they ask is that I keep my eyes open and my heart alert for some "holy visitation," for a new insight from God.

The Homesick Heart came upon me as a series of "Aha's!" beginning with the three years I spent studying and meditating on the incarnation and death of Jesus Christ. When I began, my desire was to be gripped by the great truths of the faith. I realized that being *gripped* by the great truths was not the same thing as *grasping* them. Being gripped is a work of God. I realized that all I could do was put myself in the way of truth through study and prayer. I asked God to do a true work in me. Then I stood in the light, expectant.

As I came time after time to these two great doctrines—Jesus' incarnation and death—a large and radiant sense impressed itself on me. More wonderful than any of the insights that emerged from my study was the overwhelming sense that God does not seek us dispassionately. And I found that I could not handle Jesus' incarnation and death merely as historical realities or spiritual blessings. His coming among us and His death on the Cross were expressions of a loving and a longing heart. The loving part was nothing new, but I had never before considered His *longing*.

That God longs for us doesn't diminish Him. He longs because He loves us, not because He has a need. From His intense desire for us, God makes one overture after another. He reveals Himself to us in multitudinous ways because we could never find the One who is eternal, infinite, invisible, and holy on our own. He willingly stripped Himself of all privilege as God to become a man and, then, to die on the Cross. All the works and gifts of God descended and continue to descend on us from the heart of a longing God.

As I ponder His longing, I face my own longing with new interest and wonder: Are our longings reflections of His longing? Are the longings that undeniably touch all humans sent to awaken us to seek God? Is conversion best understood in terms of our longing? Do the longings that continue even after we make intimate connection with God remain within us for a purpose? How can we cooperate with our longings that they might accomplish their work in us? And finally, What is the intended end for a people plagued with longing?

This book grew out of my attempt to explore these questions for myself. During the nearly ten years I've worked on this book, I've pondered the dilemma: How do I find words to speak of something as profoundly mysterious as longings, homesickness, and soul hunger? How do I communicate the "Aha's!" of spiritual truth? Certainly not by clinical means. This theme defies microscope and formula. A teaching style isn't appropriate either. "Aha's!" aren't taught. The soul simply receives revelation or it doesn't. I've wrestled down to the very deadline of this manuscript trying to communicate clearly without violating the subject, without divesting an incomprehensible wonder of mystery.

The style I chose to convey something of the wonder I experienced may take some getting used to in places. For this reason, I make an unconventional request: *Stand in the light, expectant!*

The subject is not new or foreign to us. We all long for something. We live with the hungers of our hearts, but we rarely look them in the eye. Undoubtedly, our lives would be richer if we did.

Perhaps, as you consider my ponderings on the longing of God and get a glimpse of my own longing, you will more fully understand and cherish the hungers so graciously implanted in your heart. Perhaps reading this book will make you more sensitive and responsive to the God who longs for you. Perhaps you will recognize your longings for what they are and cooperate with them in deeper ways that they might do their holy work in you. Perhaps this will be an "Aha!" book for you.

That is my prayer.

*It is well worth being lost in the fog for a little while
for the sake of being found at last and carried home.*

—T. Everett Harré

PART 1

OUR HUMAN LONGING

CHAPTER ONE

THE HOMESICK HEART

YEARNING FOR A PLACE

WE'VE NEVER SEEN

—

Like Adam,

we have all lost Paradise;

and yet we carry Paradise around

inside of us in the form of a longing for,

almost a memory of,

a blessedness that is no more,

or the dream of a blessedness

that may someday be again.[1]

Frederick Buechner

—

We were house-hunting in the Seattle area when I saw it—an old house in a modest and declining neighborhood. A full porch embraced the front and at one end of the porch a swing drifted slightly with the breeze. As we walked up the porch steps, I pictured myself on that swing. In my mind, purple clematis climbed the trellis and I sat surrounded with books, sipping a glass of iced tea. By the time we got to the front door my imagination was fully engaged.

I whispered to my husband, "I don't want to influence you, but I *love* this house."

After a tour, infatuation became committed love.

It's been fourteen years since I first loved that house, and it still calls to me. We never lived there because the wiring in the basement was held in place by clothespins, the foundation was crumbling, and the roof needed replacing. Strange that a house I never lived in calls to me like an ancestral home. But aren't we all homesick for a home we've never lived in? Don't we all feel the call of a home we've never seen?

My homesickness is not for a piece of geography, but the term *homesickness* comes close to describing the longing I feel. A real, almost palpable, yearning attends me. It makes no difference that I grew up in a home where I was loved and I have a rich life as an adult; my yearnings whisper, "There should be more." I sense that I was meant to be more . . . better, that I was meant to live in a world of beauty, justice, and love; that I have a capacity to love and be loved that even my deepest loves and friendships can't satisfy. I struggle to find ways to express it. All I know is that it feels like homesickness.

Contemporary writer Peter Matthiessen was speaking of this same kind of longing when he wrote, "I already had what Kierkegaard called 'the sickness of infinitude,' wandering from one path to another with no real recognition that I was embarked upon a search, and scarcely a clue as to what I might be after. I only knew that at the bottom of each breath there was a hollow place that needed to be filled."[2]

No one escapes. In every person resides a vague sense that something is missing. Built into the very constitution of our being is some unshakable—though indistinct—awareness of something we've almost known. We feel the loss of what was meant to be.

This "almost memory" is a fleeting, evasive thing. Like the name we know but can't recall, it eludes us. It wafts past us with all the sweetness and promise of an answer to our longings. The taste and aroma of it vanishes like a vapor. If it tarried but a moment more, perhaps we could identify it. Our hearts leap and grasp for it, but we cannot hold on to it.

We can't adequately define our longings, but we can't deny them either. We call them by different names, attribute them to various sources, and try to alleviate them in a multitude of ways. It is troublesome to be so anonymously haunted.

Although our yearning doesn't come clearly labeled, the German intellectual Hermann Hesse agrees with me that it feels like homesickness. Hesse has the Steppenwolf admit, "A secret yearning for something homelike drives me."[3] In fact, homesickness drives Hesse's entire book. And not this book only. In much of what I read, I sense that underneath the joy, wretchedness, lust, or melancholy brought to life on the pages, a yearning unmentioned smolders.

I am comforted; I don't long alone. Others know the yearning and choose to express it as homesickness too. They, too, speak of the vague, sweet agony of it, the heaviness and lightness of it. Frederick Buechner, in this penetrating vignette about Eve, captures something of the nagging loss I feel.

> It was only once in a while at night, just as she was going off to sleep with all her usual defenses down that her mind drifted back to the days when, because there was nothing especially important to do, everything was especially important; when too good not to be true hadn't yet turned into too good to be true; when being alone was never the same as being lonely. Then sad and beautiful dreams overtook her which she would wake up from homesick for a home she could no longer even name, to make something not quite love with a man whose face she could not quite see in the darkness at her side.[4]

The summons comes to us in an alien land far from the Garden designed for us. This unfriendly landscape is not so much distinguished by weeds and pollution as by an atmosphere that distorts our perceptions. Like Samson who fell under Delilah's spell while she snatched him bald, we mistake the nature of our longings and look to the physical world to satisfy them. But we find that even the best parts of our lives leave the empty space at the core of our being still yearning.

Unfortunately, when logic demands that we ask ourselves hard questions about the nature of our longings, we often redouble our speed toward futile goals. Like Samson, the truth that should be obvious eludes us and we again lay our heads in the lap of empty promise. We call our longings by incorrect names and assume wrong solutions. C. S. Lewis wrote, "What does not satisfy when we find it, was not the thing we were desiring."[5]

I hear the call for home in my best moments as well as in my loneliness and disappointments. These indescribable, bittersweet yearnings often broadside me. The most unexpected stimuli may trigger a brief flood of sorrow and desire, and my soul suffers an unaccountable craving.

C. S. Lewis understood perfectly the homesick feelings I have such trouble articulating when he penned this passage in *Till We Have Faces*. In his book, when Orual comes to comfort her beloved sister Psyche, who is about to be sacrificed on the mountain, Orual confronts a most unexpected wedge. This final meeting between sisters is spoiled, not by overwhelming sorrow, not by dread, but by desire. Orual is not prepared for the rapturous anticipation Psyche expresses.

Psyche says, "It was when I was happiest that I longed most. It was on happy days when we were up there on the hills, the three of us, with the wind and the sunshine. . . . Do you remember? The colour and the smell, and looking across at the Grey Mountain in the distance? And because it was so beautiful, it set me longing, always longing. Somewhere else there must be more of it. Everything seemed to be saying, Psyche come! But I couldn't (not yet) come and I didn't know where I was to come to. It almost hurt me. I felt like a bird in a cage when the other birds of its kind are flying home."

Psyche continues, "The sweetest thing in all my life has been the longing . . . to find the place where all the beauty came from . . . my country, the place where I ought to have been born. Do you think it all meant nothing, all the longing? The longing for home?"[6]

What is the root of our homesickness? Where does this homing instinct come from, and where is it trying to lead us? Is this yearning as universal as it seems?

I've read that every Eskimo baby is born with a blue Mongolian spot at the base of his spine. That dab of blue flesh documents his ancestry. A patch of blue on an Eskimo's bottom affirms his lineage. Do the longings in the human heart verify our humanity and descent? Is our homesickness our Mongolian spot? Are our irrefutable and universal longings the most accurate indication of our origin, purpose, and destiny? Could it be that our longings tell us more about ourselves as humans than any other thing about us?

⟶

The Buddha sat under the pines in Katmandu and taught that our cravings are the source of our sorrows and that suffering would be eliminated and peace attained if we extinguished our longings. But are our longings the problem, or are they the sherpas to lead us home? Do we lose our best help in finding what we seek when we attempt to douse these warmly burning desires?

Our longings are not a curse. Their pestering persistence is an evidence of supreme possible good. Our longings are meant to keep us searching. If longings exist, then that which will fulfill them must exist. That sense propels us—there must be more. The longings demand it.

If we understand our longings, we will kiss them on both cheeks. Our longings come not for our misery but for our good.

Yet a curse has fallen upon humanity because of sin. We were expelled from the Paradise created for us. But along with that loss, we feel a sense of hope. And the sense of loss and hope are nearly inseparable. Just as we know something has been lost, we feel it must not be lost to us forever. The air carries a promise, a hope, an assurance that it may be recovered.

That I am homesick for a home I've never seen would be preposterous if I had no glimpse, no foretaste, of that home. The home I seek is not here, yet in the hearth fire and the freshly made bed I feel pangs of homesickness for a home beyond my experience. I can't describe this home, but the seeds of recognition are planted within me.

Our unknown home calls to us continually, sending impassioned messages full of clues and yearnings. The clues are varied, personal, and fleeting. Graham Greene wrote, "And they mean nothing at all to another human being than the man who catches them."[7]

For me, the call comes and disappears before I can name it. When it comes, my spirit rises to something— a melody, a scent, a brush of the wind against my skin.

In the children's classic *The Yearling*, Marjorie Kinnan Rawlings describes the call to the young protagonist in this way: "A mark was on him from the day's delight, so that all his life, when April was a thin green and the flavor of rain was on his tongue, an old wound would throb and a nostalgia would fill him for something he could not quite remember."[8]

Some might attribute this to merely physical or chemical phenomena. But all of us, religious or not, whatever culture or beliefs, *know* that something unexplainable, but nevertheless real, happens to us unbidden.

Pulitzer prize-winning author Annie Dillard wrote:

> When Ella Fitzgerald sang, "There's someone I'm trying so hard to forget—don't you want to forget someone too?," these facile, breathy lyrics struck me as an unexpectedly true expression of how it felt to be alive. This was experience at its most private and inarticulate: longing and loss. "It's the wrong time, it's the wrong place, though your face is charming, it's the wrong face." I was a thirteen-year-old child; I had no one to miss, had lost no one. Yet I suspect most children feel this way, probably all children feel this way, as adults do; they mourn this absence or loss of someone, and sense that unnamable loss as a hole or hollow moving beside them in the air.[9]

You know it, too. Sometimes it happens at a sunset. Or it may come, unexplainably, as you hear a combination of musical notes or read some phrase that contains a wondrous kernel of truth. However it comes, the call is a silvery shaft of sunlight bestowed on you through a door slightly ajar, a faint echo of a conversation originating in eternity.

If we could hear that conversation, we would understand our longings and the reason they cannot be assuaged here. From that first whisper of summons, uttered perhaps before our birth, God sends out the breath of His yearning. This call from God touches the supreme interest of the soul and our soul rises up in response, even though we usually misname the quickening.

The arousal mounts up from the infinite abyss of the soul. This is a peculiar hunger because we are made in the image of God (Genesis 1:26-27) with a place and capacity for God. Saint Augustine said it well when he said that God made us for Himself and that our hearts find no rest until they rest in Him.

In the most hallowed recesses of our person, we were made for relationship with God. God has left His imprint on our inner man like fossil impressed in rock. "He has also set eternity in the hearts of men; yet they cannot fathom what God has done from beginning to end" (Ecclesiastes 3:11).

We cannot comprehend eternity. We function, birth to death, governed by the boundaries of time. Though we live in an obviously finite world, something in our hearts aspires to the infinite. We have a sense, an inkling, a foreboding, that life on earth may be merely a parenthetical phrase within an eternal context. Our physical being operates in the temporal realm, but our spirit belongs to another reality. The human heart holds a secret. If we could read the language of our heart—an undeciphered hieroglyph etched in the deepest part of our being—we would find an implanted assurance of other realms.

Just as we look for a home on earth to shelter us physically, we sense in our spirits that we were made for a Home of another order. No matter how perfect our circumstance, how perfect our home here on earth, we realize that no home here fits the shape of our yearning.

—

God, holy and complete, why did You open this door of longing to me? Yet, I know. You made me for Yourself out of Your desire. Cause my longing to mingle with Your own. Stir my homesick heart and lead me Home.

PART 2

GOD'S LONGING

CHAPTER TWO

GOD LONGS TOO

OUR LONGING

IS BUT A SHADOW OF HIS

Still with unhurrying chase,

And unperturbed pace,

Deliberate speed, majestic instancy,

Came on the following Feet,

And a Voice above their beat.[1]

Francis Thompson

I taught a fourth grade class of underachievers, discipline problems, and low abilities. I loved these kids and yearned for them to know something better than the dark clouds building on their horizons. I was told that one boy and his brother stole bikes and their father helped them paint them to disguise their appearance. Another boy came to school tired because his mother's boyfriend was sleeping off a drunk on his bed. There was anger and frustration in many that stemmed from repeated failure. Those who wanted something better had to fight their way clear of peers who sneered at honest attempts to learn.

I was young, enthusiastic, and idealistic—a quavering combination—and totally unprepared for what I found in that fourth-grade classroom. I came ebullient with ideas to enrich their world and learning, but found enough resistance to severely curtail my soaring. With wings clipped, I mourned over my class. I ached, literally. I lost weight. I slept poorly. I anguished in examination and reexamination of each day's class. I searched myself, the material, and the individuals in the class for some clue to clear the impasse. The anguish I felt did not grow from trauma to my personal ambition as their teacher, but from the portent, all heavy and black, accumulating above their heads. I feared the best of life would elude them, not only as fourth graders, but in all of time and eternity.

When I read the Old Testament phrase, "Yet the LORD longs to be gracious to you" (Isaiah 30:18), I recognized something of the pained yearning I felt. The word *yet* holds in tension both the desire to do them good and the frustration of having hands securely tied by their resistance.

I hear that same frustration in Jesus' words, "O Jerusalem, Jerusalem, you who kill the prophets and stone those sent to you, how often I have longed to gather your children together, as a hen gathers her chicks under her wings, but you were not willing" (Matthew 23:37).

I knew something of stretching out hen wings, of calling needy chicks and watching them turn and mince and peck at the edge of the precipice. My students were full of longing, too, but their longings and mine ran on seemingly parallel tracks—within sight of one another, but never to meet.

I longed; and I did what I could. My heart was raw and tender, my dreams rebuffed. I would seek again, tomorrow, some new expression, some innovative plan, some fresh enterprise, to span the gap between their longings and mine.

—

Who can deny that the human race is universally beset with yearning? The astonishing revelation comes when another longing surpasses our own, surging past us with a trembling velocity. God doesn't turn His back on our longings in indifference; His longings, a greater, graver, holier yearning than anything we know, unfurl bird wings in solemn invitation.

His longing, unlike ours, emanates from a selfless love, not from any need on His part. God is complete in Himself. But when He created people, He opened a door of pain and longing.

Dame Julian, a fourteenth-century contemplative, said that just as God is a God of compassion and pity, He is a God of thirst and longing. I think she is right.

In an amazing display of longing, God takes the initiative to make Himself known. He must. He is invisible, infinite, eternal and divine. Humanity can know nothing of Him apart from His gracious Self-revelation. He demonstrates the enormity of His love and longing in the Herculean lengths to which He goes to make Himself known.

Years ago, when my friend Louise would visit, my husband would sometimes entertain her three-year-old son, Kerry, whose father was at sea with the navy. Roger explained the game Hide and Seek to Kerry. But as soon as Roger called, "Here I come," Kerry would jump out from behind the couch.

"Here I am!" Kerry would shout as he leaped into view, his arms flung exuberantly overhead.

At first Roger tried to explain to Kerry that he must stay hidden until found. But finally, and wisely, Roger concluded that Kerry had grasped the true objective of the game. The joy is not in hiding but in finding and in being found.

God says, "I revealed myself to those who did not ask for me; I was found by those who did not seek me. To a nation that did not call on my name, I said, 'Here am I, here am I.' All day long I have held out my hands to an obstinate people, who walk in ways not good, pursuing their own imaginations" (Isaiah 65:1-2).

I see the Lord standing there, like Kerry, with outstretched arms: "Here I am. There is joy in finding Me and My joy is in being found." As far as I can tell, everywhere God is jumping out from behind couches in Self-revelation.

This morning the moon, in full glory, hangs over the Rockies. I sit at my bedroom window in semi-darkness and watch the mist-cloaked sphere through the window screening. I steady my elbow on the sill and rest my chin in cupped hand to observe the moon's carefully measured decline in the wire mesh. As the moon drops lower, the surrounding haze that softens its edges falls away, and sharp, clean, cold lines form against a matte-gray sky. Gradually a gentle pervading pink tints the scant, slanting clouds over the mountains. I've seen photos of men walking on the moon, but I can't believe it was this same moon. Not this mysterious, pallid ball, so remote and untouchable.

I wait for that moment in time and infinitude when the lower edge of the moon's circumference will touch the mountain ridge and balance perfectly in climax. Was the long night's trek across the nocturnal sky all for this brief, final show of glory? And then my lunar performer slides away, down the slippery back of the mountain—a sphere, then a blister, then a mere flicker of light through trees, like sun reflected off house windows on a distant hill, then a pale radiance in an empty sky.

I come downstairs to fix breakfast, and from the kitchen window I see the sun rise in ever-increasing intensity. Yesterday is behind me now. A new day begins. And I reflect on these two faithful witnesses to the God who wants to be known.

The sun and moon are part of God's diverse and profuse communication with humanity. He sows planets and stars in space like so many crops on earth. The picture we get of God from nature is incomplete, but every terrain and clime, every detail or horizon, whether bleak or beautiful, reveals something of Him. Everywhere God is trying to startle us awake that we might see Him.

God formed the heavens and the earth with man in mind: "For this is what the LORD says—he who created the heavens, he is God; he who fashioned and made the earth, he founded it; he did not create it to be empty, but formed it to be inhabited—he says: 'I am the LORD, and there is no other. I have not spoken in secret, from somewhere in a land of darkness; I have not said to Jacob's descendants, 'Seek me in vain'" (Isaiah 45:18-19).

God's primary intent is to reveal Himself, not to hide; to speak, not to withdraw. God did not put in man the need for Him and then retreat to a dark corner of an impossible maze. In His essential nature, God is a communicator.

Everywhere a longing God attempts to unfold some glory of Himself in smaller glories that our finite minds can receive. Once I recognize these mini-revelations, I find that no matter how wondrous the attribute or aspect of God disclosed, I am most moved by the act of revelation itself. That God, holy and majestic, puts aside His dignity and manifests Himself in the most ordinary kinds of things astonishes me.

God not only condescends to make Himself known, He expresses divine mysteries in terms concrete and familiar to make the truth accessible to our limited human minds. Like a father who stoops to look his toddler in the eye, God considers our limitations.

God typifies, interprets, and explains Himself in numerous similes, metaphors, and analogies. Does it strike you as funny and touch you deeply that God would tell us He is like a chicken, a gardener, a nursing mother, a rock? I suppose Athanasius, a fourth-century believer, was right when he said, "Just because God cannot tell us *what He is,* He very often tells us *what He is like.*"[2]

Perhaps God feels the limitation of the poet who struggles to make an inadequate language express His thoughts. "There were no words for his images. He would have to invent new ones, stretch the dry withered skin of language until it could hold the flesh and blood of life — and the white breath of vision."[3]

The psalmist stretches words almost to the breaking point when he writes, "He will cover you with his feathers, and under his wings you will find refuge; his faithfulness will be your shield and rampart" (Psalm 91:4).

It would be ludicrous, even blasphemous, to say that God is a bird or a shield. But God reveals His longing heart as He parcels out His magnificence in little packages that only imperfectly represent Him so that we might know Him.

—

Whenever my husband and I travel in the southeastern part of the United States, I notice the porch furniture and think of God's longing. Two or more chairs stud every porch. Wicker, cane, twig, wood, and wrought iron — all monuments to the social arts. Once I counted twelve rocking chairs on one large porch. No wonder the South has produced so many of our country's greatest writers. Where better than a porch for a storyteller to finely hone his craft?

Everybody knows that a good story engages the listener more totally than a great speech, that an hour on the porch is better than an hour in the classroom. So God tells tales of love and longing. His stories detonate with tremendous force. I stand beneath the mushroom-shaped cloud and feel the fallout of emotion. The prodigal son— a story of waste, purposelessness, jealousy . . . and love (Luke 15:11-32). Hosea and Gomer—a tale of degradation and restoration (Hosea). One tells a story about a rebellious child and the other about an unfaithful spouse—relevant topics for any generation.

A restless, angry son throws away a good life at home and ends up eating with the pigs. A wife, with lust insatiable, strikes out on her own and finds herself on the auction block. Common stories both. The uncommon part is that the heartbroken father and the wronged husband play God's part.

To illustrate something of His desire for us, God commanded Hosea to marry a woman unworthy of him. Gomer was unloving, ungrateful, and unfaithful. Hosea loved and provided for her, but she was hell-bent on looking elsewhere for love. Despite her ingratitude and frantic and brazen promiscuity, God tells Hosea, "Go, show your love to your wife again, though she is loved by another and is an adulteress. Love her as the LORD loves the Israelites, though they turn to other gods and love the sacred raisin cakes" (Hosea 3:1).

This is the account of a real woman on a fast and slippery self-destructive slide, a woman ravaged and dissipated by loose living, a woman staggering in the muck and mire of poor choices. Gomer, a shell of the woman she could have been, is bought out of prostitution by her husband and taken home again as his wife.

Neither Gomer nor the prodigal son could see how good they had it at home. It was some craving within that drove them wantonly on. This is the human condition:

unsatisfied, restless, driven by some sense that life is better on the other side of the fence.

The high point of these stories, for me, is that just when I expect God to lob in hand grenades, He runs to His son, falls on his neck with kisses, and kills a fatted calf for a dinner celebration. When I expect Him to say, Serves you right, or, Fry in hell, He buys Gomer out of slavery and makes her a bride again.

God's longing leaves me disturbed and embarrassed for Him. I don't want Him to make a fool of Himself over Gomer or a delinquent boy. I don't want to see Him standing there with red, swollen eyes or an aching lump in His throat.

And then He turns those blood-rimmed eyes toward me.

Drapes the robe around my shoulders.

Slips the ring on my finger.

And turns *me* toward Home.

In these dramas, God thwarts efforts to find satisfaction in illegitimate ways. He says of Gomer, "Therefore I will block her path with thorn bushes; I will wall her in so that she cannot find her way. She will chase after her lovers but not catch them; she will look for them but not find them" (Hosea 2:6-7). All this that she might say, "I will go back to my husband as at first, for then I was better off than now" (verse 7).

The same pattern occurs in the prodigal son's story. A severe famine hit. His money gone, he fed the pigs and went hungry himself. "When he came to his senses, he said, 'How many of my father's hired men have food to spare, and here I am starving to death! I will set out and go back to my father and say to him . . .'" (Luke 15:17).

God's longing, as well as our longing, resonates in

these stories of agonizing loss. Good things and good circumstances cannot fill our yearning place. Incredible as it sounds, the good life stirs the fires of longing as powerfully as hard times, because we have not yet found what we are longing for. We race off after lovers, wealth, power, freedom, and emptiness. Perhaps we are thwarted, bruised, and stripped to bring us to our senses, to turn us around. In all this, God waits that He might throw a party for the sheer joy of having us home again.

It seems that God will try almost anything to get our attention. He shows fragments of Himself in every imaginable way. Our God jumps out from behind the couch or waits on the porch to spin another tale of truth and yearning for His class of "going-nowhere" fourth graders, rebellious sons and unfaithful wives. Is there no end to the things He'll try to move us toward Home?

—

Lord, Your longing takes me by surprise and moves me. You want me to know You, but You never loom or blare. You come quietly, gently, softly, delivering parcels of Yourself and drawing me into Your longing with stories. Forgive me, I have such trouble looking beyond my own longing to see Yours. Open my heart to Your longing, O God.

CHAPTER THREE

A WORD
OF LONGING

THE WORD BECAME FLESH

AND LIVED AMONG US

While all things were in quiet silence

and that night was in the midst

of her swift course,

Thine almighty Word

leaped down from heaven

out of Thy royal throne.[1]

Malcolm Muggeridge

A s a child, I woke Christmas morning with my heart revved to a high-pitched whine. With heightened and surging senses, my brother and I called from bed for permission to get up and get dressed—a Christmas rule. Our parents had the machinery of the holiday finely tuned and legislated that we dress and make our beds before beginning our celebration. One year we slept in our clothes in one bed to shorten those nerve-twitching preliminaries.

Our family's particular ritual of standing a stark naked tree in the living room on Christmas eve for Santa Claus to decorate made Christmas morning especially startling to the senses. That first blast of color and fragrance, glitter and sparkle, was heady and intoxicating.

I remember standing all jittery and tingly behind curtained French doors, as full of nerves as a man waiting for his bride's advance down the aisle. When I could contain the jarring anticipation no longer, I succumbed and pulled aside the curtain for a peek. This glimpse, though a mere shaving of effulgence, sent a quiver of excitement through me.

Undeniably, I expected some magic at Christmas. But after the initial jolt of evergreen, glowing lights, and opened gifts, I sat in the rubbish of wrapping paper feeling a pang of disappointment. In the midst of plenty and wonder, I felt a strange disillusionment and emptiness. Underneath the hype there was a grieving like death. I mourned because even in this scintillating season, this season of historical and cultural richness, of family, friends, and abundant plunder, something was missing.

Was I expecting too much?

—

Perhaps it's that we settle for far too little. I wonder if we've become so acquainted with disappointment in this life that we acquiesce, accept emptiness, and even expect it. And then at special times, like Christmas, we raise our hopes and dare to believe that this time we'll get something more than hugs and presents. "Maybe this year," you say. I wonder.

The notion that there is something more to Christmas always seems to tremble in the background. We, and this notion, take a few steps forward holding a scalpel and microscope. *What happens if we probe, if we dissect, push, and squeeze for deeper meaning?* This notion is the prod, the prompting to exploratory surgery. It says, "Bring out this holiday that raises our expectations. Cut away. Discard the extraneous. Make your incision here in the gut of the Christmas story."

I stand in surgical greens and mask before the prologue of John's gospel, a poetic passage that strings together the bare bones of Christmas. I make an incision. I step up to this tiny rend, this knothole in the fence, and peer into eternity. Silently I put my stethoscope to the opening. I sense a pulse throbbing, a heart breaking, a holy homesickness. I am incapable of fully grasping what I see, but I feel the breath of the endless past and the boundless future. These eighteen verses force me to look beyond a baby in a manger to the eternal heart of a longing God.

The poetry begins—cosmic realities stacked, compressed, concentrated, austerely waiting to explode. "In the beginning was the Word."

What is this eternal Communication? Who is this

One who tells us moving stories, who reveals Himself as mother bird? Who is this Logos that jumps from behind the couch?

I clip an artery and apply a hemostat. The Greek verb tenses used in the poem indicate that He is timeless, continuous, that there never was a time when He didn't exist.

"And the Word was with God, and the Word was God. He was with God in the beginning."

I inspect the vital organs. The ancient poem says this Word created all that is, and that He is life and the light of men. Creator. Light. Life.

What is it we crave, if not life? Not our life that comes with the seeds of death embedded in it. But real life, true life, pure LIFE.

I trace the veins and arteries back to that pulsating lifegiver the way explorers walk upstream to discover headwaters that feed tributaries. And I find the Word, the Fountainhead of Life.

The poem goes on: "The Word became flesh and lived for a while among us."

How tragic if the Word behind these words should only warm us mildly like a sip of holiday punch rather than transport us to the brink and leave us staring off into the chasm of eternity and yearning. God's speaking—the Speaker and the Message spoken—lived among us. The Communication crossed some invisible borderline between the worlds, came in a body and lived among us in common clothes. The Eternal One left His Home and pitched His tent beside ours—a sacrifice hard to imagine. What amazing gravitational force would keep the Eternal One in our camp?

Perhaps African novelist Camara Laye was wondering

the same thing when she described the frail, adolescent king who looked like he might float up into the sky if it weren't for all the gold bracelets encircling his arms and legs. The beggar who serves as a guide in this adventure remarks that if the king weren't so heavily weighed down, there would be nothing to keep him among them. The beggar explains to the European in the story that while gold is always only gold to white men, "Gold may also be one of the signs of love, that is, the purest kind of love. That is the sort of gold that holds the king a prisoner, and that is why his arms are so heavily laden."[2]

—

I return to my exploratory surgery. I palpate the tissue. The imagery in the Greek of God pitching His tent among us would not be lost on the Jewish reader. In the Old Testament, God told the people to provide a tent within their camp where He might meet with them. This Tent of Meeting and, later, the Tabernacle were closely linked in the Jewish mind with God's presence with them. These tents were God's idea. In Christmas, He comes, once again, weighed down with love and longing to share our encampment.

—

You know the Christmas narrative. A virgin is pregnant. The text says, "What is conceived in her is from the Holy Spirit. She will give birth to a son, and you are to give him the name Jesus, because he will save his people from their sins" (Matthew 1:20-21). The virgin ends up delivering her baby in a stable in Bethlehem. God comes in infant flesh fresh from the womb.

This occurrence rides on the crest of a tidal wave of paradox and incongruity. Everywhere the common and supernatural are borne along together in unimaginable union. The force of the wave explodes upon us, either shattering and enfolding us in the torrent, carrying us forward and embracing us to its bosom, or else thundering so monstrously that we plug our ears, struggle to our feet, and seek to free ourselves from its implications.

The elements of the Incarnation cannot be fully defined or integrated. That Heaven and earth should converge in Bethlehem is fired with complexities beyond human understanding. As in no other event, Heaven and earth meet in some formerly unknown territory—a meeting between the worlds. Angels and shepherds face on a hillside outside Bethlehem, and who is to say which were the most amazed by it all. A heavenly sign in the ancient sky signals the birth of a king, and Magi from the East caravan to that Bethlehem corridor where Heaven and earth touch unexpectedly and irrepressibly. The distance between Heaven and earth was never less, the distinction never greater.

Nowhere is the fallout from this convergence more startling than in the phrase "with child through the Holy Spirit" (Matthew 1:18). What incongruity! With child. In a family way. Pregnant.

From the beginning, every generation knows what it is to be with child. Not to take away from the magic and miracle of birth, but pregnancy is common. Women of every era in history, dull and bright women, kind and severe women, responsible and irresponsible women have been with child.

The verdict, "You're pregnant," brings feelings of bounding joy or trapped desperation. For those who want their baby, the experience of carrying a child is inexpressible: swelling abdomen, ripple of interior motion, protruding fetal knee, infant hiccup shaking mother's inner works.

"Do not be afraid, Mary, you have found favor with God. You will be with child and give birth to a son, and you are to give him the name Jesus. He will be great and will be called the Son of the Most High. The Lord God will give him the throne of his father David, and he will reign over the house of Jacob forever; his kingdom will never end" (Luke 1:30-33).

Words meant to reassure cause great upheaval. "How will this be," Mary asks the angel, "since I am a virgin?"

The angel answers, "The Holy Spirit will come upon you, and the power of the Most High will overshadow you. So the holy one to be born will be called the Son of God."

—

Who can comprehend either eternity or birth? Our minds blanch at the unfathomable magnitude of eternity—limitless, immeasurable. But is the birth of a child any less mysterious? We speak authoritatively in biological terms, but anyone who has attended a birth knows that the question "Where do babies come from?" has never been satisfactorily answered.

When eternity and birth express themselves in a stable in the Middle East, the greatest mystery of all is pushed into an unprepared world. The unknowable made knowable. The transcendent made approachable.

Borne from Heaven to be born on earth. The purity of Heaven not lessened a whit; the need of earth not ignored.

Very God, yet very man, as Athanasius said. Baby flesh.

—

A clamped artery begins to bleed unaccountably. "He was in the world, and though the world was made through him, the world did not recognize him. He came to that which was his own, but his own did not receive him" (John 1:10-11).

The situation is misdiagnosed. A wrong assessment of the facts. A symptom treated; a root problem ignored. It happens all the time. Things aren't as they look. Sometimes the very thing planted right before our eyes appears different than we expect, and we overlook the obvious. Life came to us in an infant body. Life lay in Mary's arms and drew nourishment from His creation. Life appeared and we failed to recognize Him because He looked like us.

The four gospels are eyewitness accounts of His life on earth written by close associates. They record His works, teachings, and conversations, with scant comment or interpretation. The Jesus I find there is unlike the Jesus of caricature, unlike the ethereal, floating Jesus of cinema, or the militant revolutionary Jesus of narrow social causes. He is beyond comprehension. He is thoroughly good. He burrows to the heart of an issue. He is totally impartial and not self-conscious. He never adjusts His actions to please people. He is devoid of social, cultural, or sexual bias.

Many have claimed to be God over the centuries. Emperors' palaces and insane asylums house their share of the grandly disturbed. In every era unscrupulous, deceived, or deranged men have alleged their godhood and led their misguided faithful. Time passes and no one gives serious thought to their assertions. Only in Jesus is the consideration worth entertaining.

In every reading of Jesus' gospel biographies, I am more acutely aware that though He is much like us, He is different enough that He could have come from another world. As indeed He did.

—

It doesn't bother me that stores put up Christmas decorations in October. Their motivation may be sales, but this holiday brings me face to face with the material evidence of God's longing for mankind. In this holiday God's longing takes its most tangible form. This is a holiday for touching, feeling, handling. It's a "pass-the-baby-around, sniff-his-neck, kiss-the-newborn-flesh-with-lips-hungry-for-reality" kind of holiday. A real hands-on day. God's birthday.

The Incarnation tips the scales at both ends. God with a birth date is as difficult a concept to grasp as His being eternal. The Everliving One born? He who has no beginning or ending come to earth with the same beginning and ending as all men: conception, gestation, birth, growth, and death? Yet every time we pen the date, we affirm that His birth is the pivotal point of history.

—

Earth lights its trees in December to set the world ablaze. And a blinking star atop a fir reminds me that another star once lit up Bethlehem with His longing. Majesty made man. Unmeasured glory gestating in a foreign womb. Contained. Confined. Infinite dweller on high, lofty and absolute, pushed through Heaven's birth passage, down, down, down, to earth. Squeezed from warm darkness into the blinding brightness of a sin-infected world.

Part of me delights in the mystery. The other part is dizzy with incomprehension. The Scripture texts, redolent and bright, evoke my longing and express His. I feel the same overload of awe that I knew as a girl facing the Christmas tree. I can't bring myself to pack away thoughts of His longing when I store the lights and tinsel for another year. I lean forward in anticipation.

Lord, I can't imagine the intensity of longing that would propel a Holy God into our rude and tainted world. My longing is a mere candle compared with the blinding light of longing that blazes around us at Christmas. Thank You for coming.

CHAPTER FOUR

A TOAST TO LONGING

REDEMPTION: THE PRICE OF RECOVERING WHAT WAS LOST

God's mysterious grace

could not leave man in such forlornness;

it desired to help him home.[1]

Romano Guardini

I travel across India by rail. Actually, by book. I feel the rumbling and clacking from my armchair vicariously. I gaze at India passing, page by page. My eyes lock with those of a beautiful, young woman with a jeweled nostril. Her liquid black eyes stare beneath a fiery red dot. Her sari, swirled in paisleys and embroidered gardens, reflects the complexity of her culture. The train stops in Lucknow and I observe a squatting, turbaned man selling lizards lying white underside up on a blanket—for aphrodisiacs.

Amid strange wonders I keep turning the page back to the holy man kneeling in the sand with his head buried. I flip the page back, but he doesn't come up to breathe. The caption says he's learned to slow his breathing and heartbeat to reach "moska," redemption.

Across the page, a woman in a red and gold striped sari paints something red on a bunch of finger bananas. Small jars, dishes, and urns are arranged on the beach, and flowers are strewn around. Does this have something to do with redemption too?

It seems redemption is a strange thing. I read on. A deceased Hindu believes he can halt his incarnationary cycle and ensure he won't return next go-around as a gecko, or such, if his ashes are sprinkled in the most sacred of all rivers, the Ganges. There, firewood stacked high feeds the burning ghats where bodies are cremated. Sometimes bodies, half-burned, are pushed into the holy waters where the living come to drink and bathe seeking redemption.

Redemption is a word full of homesickness. Everywhere humanity seeks to be made right, to be set free, to make amends, to recover what was lost. I know of no culture without a redemption philosophy, no individual untouched by longing.

I can't get that holy man, kneeling there, bottom-up, out of my mind. Does redemption require humiliation? Certainly we all sense innately the estrangement and in a variety of ways seek to appease the gods. Whether by the most perverted form—human sacrifice—or by what might seem ludicrous or bizarre, we sense something must be done. God Himself acknowledges the estrangement—an alienation far deeper and more serious than we imagine. Perhaps none of us can understand the breadth and depth of the chasm.

We wonder, Can a holy man find redemption by burying his head in the sand for hours on end? Does an offering of finger bananas on the beach atone for sin? Will the polluted waters of the holy Ganges river effect some spiritual benefit?

How can we find the door Home? Are there many paths? Is the holy mountain laced with trails, all ending at the welcoming portal? Or is the path too steep, the trail overgrown and impenetrable, the landscape too wild and forbidding, the Enemy too formidable, the battle beyond our resources? Are the best and strongest turned aside by obstacles, disheartened and exhausted, still a great distance from the door? Perhaps without the heavy and cumbersome load we all carry, some would make it. But the weight of the burden shifts inconveniently at critical points in the climb, draining off precious energy, making demands of its own.

And all the while we hear Home calling.

Suppose the path were cleared ahead and another carried the burden. Suppose the Enemy had been defeated and the door flung open. Suppose you could take your head out of the sand, eat the bananas, die at home not scattered on the Ganges, and still find that Home you seek.

—

I close the book. My rail journey through India ends; my pondering about redemption continues. My attention shifts to another train, which tracks our longing and need. A train that brings us, deliberately and abruptly, face to face with the most convincing evidence of God's desire for us.

This train winds through our circuitous history: past our gods, our rituals, and our customs; past our funeral barges and our grand tombs. Our yearnings reverberate as the train breaks through the far mist of eternity. A headlight pierces the fog as the massive engine approaches Eden, newly cast in shadow. The train, crimson like blood, shudders and shivers as it snakes past the tree of the knowledge of good and evil. From the Garden a mournful moaning mingles with the vibration and yearning from the train.

Slowly the train crosses the valley floor and fires furnaces for the ascent of Mount Moriah. It grinds uphill, swaying gently on the curves. A ram caught in a thicket answers the train's howl. An old man and a boy wave and smile. The train stretches full length, long and lithe, as it heads into Egypt. Drought-scorched fields pass on the left and right. A large Jewish family caravans toward Pharaoh's lush greenness and plenty. The red stream rumbles on past blood-clad door posts, first-born corpses, and passes with a throbbing horde through an opened sea. Now the pace diminishes. The train meanders seemingly on an aimless track through vacant deserts. Here and there, something of interest: a rock gushing water, a bronze snake on a pole, twin stone tablets still smoldering from the finger of God.

Sweeping on, the journey continues. A scarlet thread, like a rivulet of blood, hangs from a window on the wall of Jericho. Another river is crossed without the slightest splash. The train winds past a riddle-ridden man who has lost his eyes and hair, past shepherds and kings, and a shepherd-king. The engine strums on, through lands of songs and weeping, blessing and judgment.

It hurtles through long, dark, silent years into the blinking brightness. A zealot in camel hair stands spread-legged on the tracks ahead, shouting, "Repent." The train plows ahead, through poor villages lit by a dazzling star, past second-rate hotels with No Vacancy signs, gathering speed to the place of the skull. The engine thunders and roars toward a cross erected on the tracks. A man beaten bloody, head bowed, hangs impaled there. He lifts His head and there is love and longing in His sunken eyes. Then, the shattering impact. Splinters of cross and bone and shreds of flesh explode.

We are thrust into the dead and silent blackness of a tunnel. I hear no word. The darkness, heavy and unyielding, swallows all sound. I can no longer hear the engine. Have we stopped? Will we languish forever in lightless silence?

Ahead, a glowing light grows brighter, warmer, closer. We burst into golden radiance. A large rock, rolled back from the tunnel exit, stands a solid monument to a great victory. A lamb bounds joyously ahead. Each leap higher and longer and more wildly exultant. And then, one leap carries Him out of sight into the clouds. The luminous clouds absorb Him. From that same hungry mouth, a shining dove emerges in royal descent. And the wail of the whistle and the scream from the wheels becomes laughter.

The train stops beside each of us in turn as we struggle with our heads in the sand trying to find the way Home. The conductor calls, "All aboooard." Some mysterious and extravagant grace refuses to abandon us so far from Home.

‌

We yearn for redemption, whether we acknowledge it or not, because we're infected and terminal. A hopeless sickness, contracted in Paradise, marked the body, marred the soul, and deadened the spirit. We sought to wrest from God something He hoped we'd never handle. We thought eating the fruit from the tree of the knowledge of good and evil would make us like God. Instead, through our mutiny, we planted seeds of savagery in the race. We rebelled against His warnings and found within ourselves an invasive, cancerous rebellion that obeys us no better than we obeyed God. We sought to be masters of our fate and found ourselves lashed to the mast. We desired freedom and wholeness, but found ourselves isolated, exposed, and terribly ill.

The truth is out. We are naked and incomplete physically, emotionally, and spiritually. Something nibbles away from the inside. Remnant thoughts left over from our Garden days haunt us. We try in a thousand ways to hide our nakedness, never learning that fig leaves only fuel the fires that consume us. Even in our rebellion something of our intended humanity exerts itself. The person we were created to be wails from some distant cavern of our existence. That voice won't let the dream die.

The groundwork for our redemption was laid in Egypt. After four hundred years in that land, the agony of the Israelite slaves increased day by day. Their prayers rasped and rattled in the empty dark. Their hope of deliverance slumbered heavily and their lumbering dreams of freedom could not get off the ground. They saw no evidence that help was on the way. The ceiling was low and impenetrable. They could not see into the gauzy heavens to know that God was at work. The taskmasters plowed their backs as they bucked and hunched beneath the whip, not knowing that God was preparing a table for them in the presence of their enemies.

The answer will not look as they imagine. The solutions to man's gravest problems never do. Perhaps that's why God keeps us in the dark. Who would have thought that a man on a cross would close the door on night? Likewise, the Israelite slaves in Egypt would find little solace in knowing that the answer to their prayers was a lamb.

In Egypt, a lamb for each household was taken from the sheep and goats, kept near the house, and cared for by the family until the day of slaughter. Did it gambol about comically, tilt its head quizzically, trot eagerly toward the children as they approached? Did it in short time wriggle and squirm into their affections? Did its curious eyes, dark and trusting, cause them to stare numbly for minutes or a thousand years to muster the resolve to slit its throat?

And the redemption train rushes on.

—

God, our lamb. A roaring lion, a charging bull or a soaring eagle. But not a lamb. A lamb betrayed by a friend, accused without reason, tried apart from the law, condemned maliciously, mocked, mistreated, and murdered.

"He was oppressed and afflicted, yet he did not open his mouth; he was led like a lamb to the slaughter, and as a sheep before her shearers is silent, so he did not open his mouth" (Isaiah 53:7).

—

God commanded the Jews to observe the Passover feast every year, to remember the deliverance He procured for them from slavery in Egypt so that the next generation would know God's great working for their forefathers. Year after year the prescribed ritual would take place: lambs slain, unleavened bread and bitter herbs eaten with roast lamb, explanations given to the young in their midst. They must not forget the lamb's blood that bought their redemption.

It is a most disconcerting and unnerving experience to confront the Lamb's death, not just once in awkward discomfort, but over and over again by choice. God commanded no sacrament to commemorate His birth, His miracles, His resurrection. Only His death we must remember and remember and remember.

It's Communion Sunday again, and I've come unprepared. Thoughtless. Scattered. Aware of the barnacles that build up around the heart. I never feel ready. The impurity of my heart, the unworthiness of my life, the casual approach I make to God Almighty, the irony of noticing a chipped fingernail as I reach for the cup, the agility of my mind to flit from thoughts of God's blood buying my salvation to the stray hairs on the coat draped on the pew before me. And I come and eat and remember: This is why He died.

Sensitive to our limitation and plight, God institutes the Communion meal with bread and wine that we may handle and taste. Bread pinched in fingertips, savored, swallowed, ingested and digested, becoming bone of my bone and flesh of my flesh. He is mine and I am His forever. "I no longer live, but Christ lives in me. The life I live in the body, I live by faith in the Son of God, who loved me and gave himself for me" (Galatians 2:20).

The bread is passed—small, sweet crackers, actually. I fix on one to pick up without touching another. As I focus on that trapezoid representing His body, I remember. His body made accessible to me . . . broken. By His stripes we are healed.

I eat the cracker and remember. I lift the cup in toast to my longing and to His.

The redemption train cuts through our moans. God undertakes for us. His longing bursts beyond all that is expected and safe. He proposes the Cross, the mightiest, the severest, the most radical expression of His desire for us.

How, then, do we gather up the strands of our longing and His and prepare our hearts to remember?

—

Lord, help me squarely face the depth of my need, and when I meet my yearning again in all its raw intensity, may I understand afresh how pale and dim my longing is compared to the Longing that conceived the Cross.

PART

3

MAKING
CONNECTION

CHAPTER FIVE

THE TRAGEDY OF ALMOST

PHANTOM HAPPINESS VERSUS

THE REAL SOURCE OF SATISFACTION

That I could think

there trembled through

His happy good-night air

Some blessed Hope,

whereof he knew

And I was unaware.[1]

Thomas Hardy

I wrote a fairy tale once. These tales we tell our children are sad sometimes, even morose. Hansel and Gretel were led into the dense forest and purposely lost by their own father. In another tale, the daughter of a poor man was sold away to spin gold out of straw, a quite impossible job description, and ends up in a covenant in which she may have to give her first baby to a strange old man. The story I made up strikes me sad as well.

ALMOST

Once upon a time, a princess settled back against the warm leather of the carriage seat with a sigh and unfurled a lacy fan. Faint lines had just begun to trace time's passing around lovesick blue eyes. Enthusiasm and weariness, hopefulness tinged with hopelessness, rested like a flowered shawl around her shoulders as the carriage lurched forward. Tenderly, she opened the gilt-paged book she carried called *The Princes*. With eyes aglow, she turned the well-worn pages.

Prince Cedric: a long, fine nose separated dark, spirited eyes; Prince Allain: strength and boyish charm set in a square face. Slowly she lifted the portrait to her face whispering, "Prince Allain, today you are my dream, my love, my life."

She pressed her lips to the page, then clutched the book to her bosom. Her eyes closed. In daydreams she walked hand and hand with Prince Allain along the river beneath pink blossomed boughs.

As she drew near the phantom prince in her

imagination, a real prince passed. His glistening steed carried him within feet of her carriage window. As he passed, her beauty caught his eye.

How lovely, he thought. *She must be sleeping. Perhaps she will be at the ball tonight.*

When our lovesick dreamer arrived at the Grand Hotel, preparations for the ball were being completed. She heard the band warming up as she unpacked her ball gown and folded back the silky comforters on the bed. Stacking the pillows high behind her, she lay back in the airy mound with her book, *The Princes*.

Tonight Prince Sebastian seemed the most handsome of all. She planted a violet nosegay in her breast, all velvety and fragrant, and imagined Sebastian close beside her.

Meanwhile, in the ballroom below, Prince Sebastian, himself, danced preoccupied, his eyes searching lest she should appear. Above, she lingered in love's stupor with the paper Prince Sebastian. The princess almost met the Prince and lived happily ever after.

Almost is a terrible word full of radiating implication. The swimmer almost made it to shore. The parachute almost opened in time. The princess almost met the prince and lived happily ever after. *Almost* rings with a hope dashed, a twist of possibilities that ended tragically.

Almost is a hinge from which the door can swing in or out. The swimmer almost drowned or almost made it to shore. The parachute almost opened in time or almost didn't. The great pathos in the word *almost* is the sense of being so close to either satisfaction or tragedy.

Our longings get us moving. They activate our search for that which will satisfy, but our longings can lead us anywhere. It is a tragic thing to come close and to miss Him, to be tracking and to miss the road Home. Our longings bump against the door and can lead us to that which will satisfy our search or they can lead us off on a wild-goose chase.

Our longings groan and creak with the strong language of a bared heart. But what is it we long for? We think the answer is happiness. Citizens of the United States of America have made the pursuit of happiness an inalienable right. We can't define this elusive bird of paradise, but we desire it desperately. We yearn for happiness and tread one path after another hoping to find the pot of gold. But when the paths wander off in different directions, we stand at the fork uncertain which trail to take. The pursuit of happiness never ends, because happiness is not an end. Happiness, after all, isn't what we're really longing for. Happiness is merely as far as we can see from our place here in the lowlands.

A few weeks ago, when I hiked above tree line in Estes Park, Colorado, the tundra path led upward to a deceptive horizon. The highest point of the mountain seemed just ahead, easily attainable. But each ascending step altered the horizon. New heights popped into view. Even as I paused at each counterfeit peak, I confronted a harsh dawning: It was not this height that I sought.

The most important pursuits of humans are seeking and believing. But seeking and believing are endeavors fraught with dangers. It always helps to know what you are looking for and to realize that what you seek may not look like what you expect.

Like a caged tiger restlessly pacing the length of the

enclosure, we instinctively know there must be more. Yet something within senses that even if we walked from pole to pole around the world, we would have an unmet yearning. We know that we won't find what we're starving for in Hawaii or *en Provence*. Paradise would be a poor place, after all, if that tender spot inside were bleeding still.

Our dreams erupt from the desire for love—a love beyond. We want to know human love, but human love is not enough. Our longings prowl hopefully. Driven by an undefined hunger, we can fall into two tragedies. We can seek wildly and indiscriminately, tasting every fruit, or we can retreat into dreams, enjoying phantom princes and missing the real thing.

"You're cold!"

"You're freezing!"

"You're hot! You're burning up! If it were a snake, it would bite you!"

Remember the game of Hot and Cold? One person hides an object and others hunt for it. After a while, if the person who hid the object observes that the seekers are losing heart, he gives hints.

"Iceberg! Iceberg! You're frozen solid!"

The most critical part of the game is knowing exactly what you are looking for. Is it a strand of red thread, a golf ball, or a thimble? But even then, the object may be nearly impossible to spot. The red thread may blend with other red threads in the drapery. The golf ball may lose its identity in a jar of cotton balls. The thimble may be easily overlooked if placed in the open with other sewing supplies.

In the real-life search, we may be "warm" but unfortunately miss what we are looking for. We almost find it. Longings ripple, and at times thunder through our being. Our eyes wander to and fro, here and there, hoping what we seek will be apparent when our gaze finally rests upon it. What are we looking for? How will we know it when we find it? Will it look like we expect? Is there a danger of looking right past it?

Our chief assignment on earth is to seek. But what if we look and look and only see men like trees walking? But then again, there is plenty to see. Tourists climb aboard buses and "do" London or the Louvre. We are bombarded with stimuli, but where is that which will satisfy our search?

Many hunt by trial and error in the vague hope they will stumble on the prize. Others seek with a slight advantage. They know something of what they seek. They know their longings are of a spiritual nature. They are on the right track. The prints are fresh and the scent is strong as they sniff along the beckoning trail.

In *The Wind in the Willows*, Mole plods through the woods behind Rat trying to make the Rat's hole by the river before snowfall when, "It was one of these mysterious fairy calls from out of the void that suddenly reached Mole in the darkness, making him tingle through and through with its very familiar appeal, even while as yet he could not clearly remember what it was. . . . A moment, and he had caught it again; and with it this time came recollection in fullest flood."

"Home!"[2]

When the scent of Home reaches us and pulls us up

short, we need to remember that it is this we seek. Peter Matthiessen sensed that "at the bottom of each breath there was a hollow place that needed to be filled."[3] He heard the call Home as surely as Mole did, but he turned to LSD and Eastern religions.

I've read that seventy-five million baby boomers are leading the return to organized religion. This stampede grows out of a real hunger, but many will follow the herd down church corridors and never reach Home. They will moderate their homesickness with religious diversion. Their searches may be sidetracked because they've mistaken the end. They are "getting warm," but may still end up wandering back roads mildly sedated.

How tragic to come within a breath and yet miss what we are looking for. The amusements, distractions, and troubles of life keep us moving. Even if we fritter our lives away in belittling and trifling quests, our strength goes somewhere. Our gaze attaches itself to something. Our hunger will nibble at some tidbit.

Spirituality can lead us as far astray as materialism or Epicureanism. Even when the object of our search bears a name, success is not assured.

—

The Jewish nation of Jesus' day longed for the Messiah with a searing desire. The prophet Haggai called Him the "desired of all nations." Even those outside the Jewish nation were interested in Him. A Samaritan woman with a shady past said, "I know that Messiah (called Christ) is coming. When he comes, he will explain everything to us."

Most just wanted Him to make them happy. Unfortunately, their ideas about Him prevented them from recognizing Him when He came. Most of those who stood close enough to reach out and touch Him, missed Him. During the years Jesus lived on earth it happened all the time. It still happens today.

It's easy to imagine the letdown the Jewish people felt. Jesus came bareheaded and barehanded. No crown. No army. No palace. No royal entourage. No wealth. Instead of pulling everything together, He turned everything upside down. He rearranged the pieces and introduced new meanings that wouldn't fit into the old wineskins. Instead of bringing triumphal conclusion, Jesus asked people to be born again, to step out in a shaky new beginning, to become like little children.

He wasn't what we expected. He wasn't what we wanted. Jesus was at the same time too great and too lowly to fit our picture of Messiah. Sometimes He strode too near blasphemy. Without batting an eye, He said, "I tell you the truth, before Abraham was born, I am" and "I and the Father are one" and "Anyone who has seen me has seen the Father." What do we make of a man who claims to be God?

The trouble is that He was also too common. He was born in a hick town, did carpentry work and some preaching. He claimed to be a king but refused to take political or military action of any kind. He was a man of irreconcilable extremes. His claims were too high and mighty, but when you came right down to it, He was just not high and mighty enough.

Jesus said He came to reveal the Father. The disconcerting fact is, He isn't the God we expected to find. Jesus made Himself equal with God, but served men. He said He came down from Heaven, but lived in a neighborhood.

He was at once too earthly and too other-worldly to suit our tastes.

In Jesus Christ God is revealed and hidden. In Jesus Christ we either find God or lose Him. Simeon said it would be so: "This child is destined to cause the falling and rising of many in Israel, and to be a sign that will be spoken against, so that the thoughts of many hearts will be revealed" (Luke 2:34-35).

In Jesus Christ God remains hidden in the fullest revelations of Himself. Man may always explain away whatever God reveals. God always leaves room for us to refuse Him. It must be so. And when at a point in history, God most perfectly and completely reveals Himself by becoming a human being and living among us, God leaves a space wide enough for us to drive a truck through that we might decide what we will do with Him. Some will come to Him in longing, others will stub their souls on an immovable rock. Blaise Pascal wrote, "What do the prophets say about Jesus Christ? That he will plainly be God? No, but that he is a truly hidden God, that he will not be recognized, that people will not believe that it is he, that he will be a stumbling-block in which many will fall, etc."[4]

We dream awake or asleep. Metaphorically speaking, our souls levitate above the dreary humdrum. We launch ourselves from bed or to it, to soar toward our heart's desire. We yearn to belong, to be loved and to be significant. Our dreams skirt paths looking for meaning. Jesus comes to interrupt the dream and finish it in spirit and truth. He comes that we might not fritter away our lives in pipe dreams, but that with Him we might act out the rest of the dream. In Christ, the essence of dreams becomes history, reality, and glorious hope. Life with Christ, in Christ, of Christ, is the only tolerable fulfillment for noble dreams.

—

O God, have mercy on us as we search. Deliver us from almost finding what we seek. Chant in our ear when we are close and holler, "You're freezing," when we've taken dead-end paths.

CHAPTER SIX

WHEN LONGINGS CONNECT

CONVERSION—THE MYSTERY OF

GOD INVADING A LIFE BY PERMISSION

For God does not create

a longing or a hope without

having a fulfilling reality

ready for them.

But our longing is our pledge,

and blessed are the homesick,

for they shall come home.[1]

Isak Dinesen

As I hike today, the wind toots softly the empty juice bottle protruding from my shorts pocket. The wind whips my hair, ripples my shirt, and plays a solo on my bottle. I watch the wind move methodically through the grasses like a stadium wave. It is the wind that makes this hot day bearable, that flips the pages of my book and reminds me that God moves, like the wind, inside people.

I stop to observe spring's progress. A few months ago, fires scorched great patches in the fields near our home. Now Indian paintbrush stand like fiery tongues above the spirit-filled field. At first I mourned the blackness. Then the rain and spring came, drawing forth tender green. And once spring started, one wildflower after another erupted to light and shouted to the four winds, "Where, O death, is your victory? Where, O death, is your sting?"

And the wind blows.

I've always loved a strong wind and a good tree. As a girl, when the sky boiled in deep indigo, and lightning sliced here and there, I would climb to the top of our maple and sit in a triumvirate of branches. From my throne amid wildly thrashing leaves, I would sway with tingling exhilaration until my poor mother would yell warnings and threats, her voice carried away by the moaning gale.

These trysts with nature were not unlike the wind that blew through my life. But mostly that wind came gently. I had a happy childhood and grew up feeling loved. In my teenage years, I experienced inconsequential disasters. I ran over my boyfriend with his car (unintentionally), punctured an aerosol can of silver paint (intentionally, but in ignorance), covering myself, the kitchen, four ducks ready for the oven and the backyard in silver paint. A horse ran away with me, twice, the day of the prom. I twisted both ankles severely as a result of diving off my uncontrollable mount, and I attended the dance in bedroom slippers.

Yet I also read serious writers and philosophers hoping to quiet the growing inner clamor. My philosophy was in constant evolution. Nothing seemed to work for long. I set goals and achieved enough of them to realize that accomplishment failed to keep its promise. The wind whistled in, rustling everything that wasn't battened down. An interior commotion refused to be hushed.

When I was a teenager, the wind began to roar frightfully around inside my soul. Until then, the wind had come in periodic bursts and then subsided while I caught my breath. Most often, the wind was like a rhythmic breath fluttering the pages of my longing. When a bellows blast came, my yearning was fully kindled.

During my senior year of high school, a teacher wrote a character reference for me and concluded that my morals were above reproach. Her words distressed me deeply. I fell painfully short of her assessment—and my own standards. By this time the wind was howling.

Something was missing. Something was gone awry. The wind shrieked around my inner man, rattling the windows. The love of my parents and friends was not enough. My philosophy of life refused to jell; my goals seemed as distant when reached as when anticipated. Worst of all, I could not muster the energy to live well. And most of the time I looked like a typical, healthy, miserable teenager.

The hot wind sucked away my vigor and then moved in like an arctic messenger driving snow before it in shifting mirages. My scorched and chilled soul accepted a friend's invitation to the beach for the weekend. A religious group sponsored activities for five hundred high-schoolers. I thought I could endure a little religion to get the fun. I wasn't antagonistic, just wary.

Unexpectedly, the talks confronted my inner struggle. A fresh breeze off the ocean trickled in around the edges of my soul as the speaker explored the creative and skillful ways we cover the holes in our lives. We so adeptly hide them from others, he said, that we often forget them ourselves. But as in all things, there comes a day of reckoning. Coverings are ripped away, blaring holes revealed.

That image intensified my awareness of need and yearning. A heaviness hung about me. I considered the holes in my life and, for the first time, wondered if I might be alienated from God. Could sin keep me from God? Was I irreconcilable? I sensed that some good waited close at hand. Would I be stiff-armed and butted back from ever reaching it? I stood on the outskirts of my Homeland with my hair flying and my dress snapping in the gale.

Jesus likened the wind to His Spirit's mysterious working in a life. He said, "The wind blows wherever it pleases. You hear its sound, but you cannot tell where it comes from or where it is going. So it is with everyone born of the Spirit" (John 3:8).

For over thirty years, the spirit and direction of my life has flowed from that spring weekend in Ocean City, New Jersey; my hurried kneeling, closer to a genuflection, and my bald prayer. Unquestionably, the most mysterious and significant moment of my life occurred when I was eighteen years old. Even to speak of it, my heart involuntarily beats in cadence with another world, and I believe.

I've felt the wind's first gentle rush and its continuing respiration, but to communicate it is another thing altogether. After all, how does one speak of a meeting with the wind? The blind receive sight. Water is changed to wine. The storm-ravaged sea is stilled. The sick are healed, the dead raised. The worn and tattered self becomes a little child all over again. A treasure is found in a field, or a pearl of great price comes into our possession and nothing can ever be the same again.

Jesus said, "I tell you the truth, whoever hears my word and believes him who sent me has eternal life and will not be condemned; he has crossed over from death to life" (John 5:24).

Annie Dillard wrote of finding a knotted snake skin beside a broken aquarium in the woods, "As though snake had burst through the broken side of the aquarium, burst through his ugly old skin, and disappeared, perhaps straight up in the air, in a rush of freedom and beauty."[2]

I read those words and felt that they spoke, somehow, of my conversion. New life in me, too vibrant for old wineskins, joyously exploded and left the ruptured form behind. Freedom and beauty possible in a life that knew only bondage to sin. "Therefore, if anyone is in Christ, he is a new creation; the old has gone, the new has come!" (2 Corinthians 5:17).

Conversion is the connection of God's longing and my own. It is an intimate union like the sexual union in marriage. A thing talked about in common terms, but impossible to fathom. It is a relationship entered into by mutual consent and desire.

Conversion is an event and a process. It is the initial intertwining of two that makes something new and organic. Two lives unite. Two become one. "I am His and He is mine."

Conversion is not a beginning nor an end; it is a point on a line of God's seeking me. Before I ever come to that point, a longing God has been working: wooing, whispering, stirring, coaxing, bruising, wounding. The journey is often confusing and frustrating, slow and painful. Conversion is my response to a God who loves and longs.

In a sense conversion is like the wedding day, a day of intimate connection. The groundwork for the marriage was laid before they approach the altar, and the outworking of the vows bind the rest of their lives.

Augustine's *Confessions* preserve for us his attempt to make sense of his conversion. But conversion is not a sensible thing. It is mysterious by nature, invisible and intangible like the wind—undefinable yet irrefutable. Augustine's book reads like a diary or a prayer. Every page reflects an intellect and a passion not easily pacified. Confessions expose a struggling man seeking to come to terms with the questions of his mind and the hungers in his heart. This quest propels Augustine from an uneasy religious and philosophical experimentation into the arms of a longing God. The search wrenches the very undergirding structures of his being. I ache as I read over his shoulder and feel the agitation of his pilgrimage.

I sense another pain as I turn each page: the pangs of a yearning God in search of Augustine; a God who catches the tears of Augustine's mother as she prays for her son; a God full of desire to shelter the vagrant, homeless soul in Himself; a God eager to rend the dried reptile skin and set a soul free.

The first love letter I received made my face flush as I read it. Until this letter I had remained fairly unmoved by the author's measured attention. But a love letter demands a response. Apathy is out of the question.

The connection I experienced with God that New Jersey weekend felt very much the same. Jesus' life and death pressed in on me like a passionately worded love letter. He came courting. He stood close enough that His warm breath fell on me. He whispered alluring words, but He respected my personhood.

He will not rape; He will not violate our wills. God treats humanity, debauched and sinful as it is, with a dignity far beyond the dignity we afford ourselves or one another. No one values the sanctity of our will and affection more than He does.

He calls to us. We can do no more than turn. The distance is immense. Then God Himself closes the gap, bridges the chasm, and floods in. Conversion—the mystery of God invading a life by permission.

In mutual longing, we make a spiritual bond with God. This vital connection with God cannot be purchased with wealth or acquired by deftness. Nothing we have or are helps one bit. Everything rests with some mysterious working in the heart, some gracious uniting of our longings with the longing of God, some unimaginable kindness effected for us and in us.

I imagine conversion like the figures of Adam and God from Michelangelo's Creation of Adam on the ceiling of the Sistine Chapel in Rome. Both figures recline facing one another, each with an arm outstretched to the other, index fingers nearly touching. Clearly, God is the initiator. Whatever takes place originates in the mind and heart of God. His outstretched arm prompts a reciprocal response. His gracious overture evokes an awareness of longing.

Just as God created Adam from His own desire and purpose, conversion is some reaping of His working in the soil of our lives and in the atmosphere around us. His finger extends toward us. He leans and strains in our direction. And if, like the young bride in the Song of Songs we see His hand through the latch opening, and our heart begins to pound for Him, and we rush to open the door (Song of Songs 5:4-5) and our fingertips touch: conversion. Whatever happens at the synapse starts a new life. As fingers meet at creation, fingers meet again and something wonderful and new occurs.

Augustine kept bad company. As a teenager he was ashamed only if he appeared more virtuous and innocent than his companions. He worked at evil, and where he fell short, he concocted vivid tales to ensure his notoriety and place.

One night, very late, sixteen-year-old Augustine and his friends stripped a neighbor's tree of pears and tossed them to the pigs. This incident deeply disturbed Augustine. Why the craving to steal when he had no desire for pears? Why this act of waste when he felt no hatred for his neighbor? What lurid thing inside him gave him delight in mischief? What fires of camaraderie compelled him to do in company things he would not do alone? What was this strange inebriation that wickedness itself brought pleasure?

Twelve years after the pear tree incident, Augustine's soul upheaval climaxed under a fig tree in his garden. Augustine desired God. The prayers of his mother and the lives of godly men he knew, men he heard about, and men he read about, inflamed his heart. He longed to be set free and yet he loved to be bound.

"Grant me chastity and continence, but not yet,"[3]

Augustine prayed tongue in his cheek and with an ache in his heart. Such was the battle-torn field of his life.

"I was bound by the iron chain of my own will. The enemy held fast my will, and made of it a chain, and had me bound tight with it. For out of the perverse will came lust, and the service of lust ended in habit, and habit, not resisted, became necessity."[4]

The jaws of the trap snapped shut, the teeth meshed tightly and the spring was too strong for escape. Augustine's will, the pirate of his person, stood defiant and mutinous with a foot on Augustine's neck. Augustine wrote, "But I was mad for health, and dying for life."[5]

Aren't we all?

Augustine and his friend Alypius walked into the garden far from the house. In turmoil of soul, Augustine wrestled with his will. The battle stormed. Augustine broke away from his friend and collapsed beneath a fig tree, giving vent to bitter tears. As he wept, he heard a child's sing-song voice, "Pick it up; read it." He returned to the spot where Alypius sat, took up the Bible, and read where his eye fell. In words from God, Augustine felt the chain snap.

Conversion . . . connection. It is the journey from the pear tree to the fig tree. The old family tree is hacked down and a new ancestry planted on earth ascends into Heaven. No longer heir to Adam and Eve and Mom and Dad. A new family tree sprouts and I am a tender, green shoot on a lower branch. The trunk has names carved in the bark—a living graffito. Father. Jesus. Holy Spirit. Lamb of God. Longing God.

On the ground, the first tree lies felled, insect infested and rotting. The leaf that bore my name on that tree has since shriveled and blown away. I was Adam's child, my parents' offspring, a child of flesh and blood, tears and diapers. I ate the unlawful fruit and felt the ground shudder under my feet. My time was limited; my fate was sealed. The wages of sin was death.

I died. But before the corpse cooled, my poor, stilled heart jump-started; my pulse surged; my eyelids flickered. New life bubbled up from an uncontaminated spring. I found myself unexpectedly seated in a Triumvirate of branches. The wind was velvet. I was newly alive and on the way Home.

Jesus calls to a homesick creation, "The kingdom of God is near." The answer to our most fundamental longing, the haven for our deepest insecurities, the theater for our wildest dreams, the balm for our misery, the Home we seek, whether we know it or not, is near. The summons resounds in ever-widening circles of promise. The call is uttered in urgency: Do not delay. Now is the hour of salvation. Near may be nearer than can be imagined—too near to control or manipulate. So near that a moment later than now may be too late.

The Kingdom of Heaven is within touching distance. Stretch forth a finger. The Kingdom hovers close at hand, but you will never see it or enter it unless you are converted.

—

Father, I tremble in wonder when I remember that point in my personal history when my longings and Yours connected. Thank You for not leaving me to myself. Thank You for sending Your wind to call me Home.

CHAPTER SEVEN

THE CAVE OF NOW

THE HOLY SPIRIT:

OUR DEPOSIT OF FUTURE BLISS

I had the idea that it might be wonderful if we could find a world where we could hold on forever to the good feelings we get from a story or a song, keep those feelings inside ourselves forever instead of having them only for fleeting moments. We hear a song or read a story, and the good feelings we get don't remain inside us. We are either anticipating them, or we've had them and they're gone. We never experience them as now. Do you know what I mean? I'm writing a story about a little girl who discovers a cave where there is a lasting now.[1]

Chaim Potok

Propped up in bed reading and rereading lines of a poem, I savor the taste of the words and the sound of the rhythms. Most of all, I relish the link of common experience. Like Elizabeth Barrett Browning, I, too, have had my head jerked back. In *Sonnets from the Portuguese*, she wrote,

> Straightway I was 'ware,
> so weeping, how mystic Shape did move
> Behind me, and drew me backwards by the hair;
> And a voice said in mastery, while I strove, —
> "Guess now who holds thee?" — "Death," I said,
>   But, there,
> The silver answer rang, — "Not death, but Love."[2]

When I believed, there was no question in my mind that I had been apprehended by Love. It was the pleasantest kind of trauma, but trauma nonetheless. What had I been apprehended for? For salvation, I divined. For the Kingdom. For eternal life. For another world. For Heaven. It all sounded faraway and remote. Was I so passionately taken for something only future? If so, my ache would deepen. Like the novelist who wanted to set her next book in the Cave of Now, a place of intense, current experience, I knew I could not stay desire until I died and went to Heaven.

I'm homesick for Life, I cried out. My yearning will not let me wait contentedly for some distant blessing. My longing can't be put on hold. I must have some reality of experience here and now, not just the promise of better days in the future. I don't expect Heaven on earth, but I must have some advance on the promise to keep me going.

My unquenchable yearning and the desire for something *now* is not so much a lack of patience as it is an insupportable need. I long for some reality of relationship with God, some measure of healing, some power toward perfection, some sense of meaning, some intimacy of relationship beyond what I've known, some blossoming in the desert, some gladness bursting into bloom, some strengthening of feeble hands and weakened knees, some placing of feet on a new highway. I must know something of what my soul aches for.

Happily, God isn't content to wait for Heaven any more than we are. When He put in us the yearning for Home, His offer was not a promise of pie-in-the-sky-by-and-by, which leaves us destitute here to get by the best we can until we get to Heaven. The call Home speaks to the now as well as the future. He gives the "first installment of future bliss" (2 Corinthians 5:5, WMS) to be enjoyed now. He has made provision for us to taste a bit of Heaven on earth, to enter into an authentic experience with Him, to know His companionship and the reality of a life of another substance—to enter the Cave of Now.

My son called yesterday. He and some friends explored a cave in the mountains. They splashed through a snow-melt stream in bathing suits and tennis shoes on a cool day to reach the cave mouth. After a crawl, they emerged in an interior room with a waterfall. Later, they put on more clothes and ate hot dogs by a fire.

Cavers entering Lechuguilla, a newly discovered cave

in New Mexico, find it even more demanding. They descend seventy feet on a rope, then climb down another eighteen feet to reach the entrance. Once in the culvert that supports the only known entrance into the cave, cavers face up to sixty-five-mile-an-hour winds as they struggle thirty feet down a ladder. Only the most experienced cavers are allowed exploration privileges in Lechuguilla as they rappel, climb, scrabble, and wriggle through the interior mapping of these virgin passages that may open into cathedral-like rooms or squeeze down into constricting dead ends. So far they have charted fifty-three miles of cave, parts of which descend over fifteen hundred feet.

This spanking new, ancient world was "discovered" in 1986 by explorers who long suspected that caves existed in the area. The telling clue came as the cave hunters felt a rush of air—the cave's breath—exhaling to adjust to barometric changes outside and coming from rubble in a ninety-foot pit. Perhaps they would still be searching if the cave had not made this gracious gesture.

I wonder. Do I enter the Cave of Now where I experience the reality of God thoroughly chilled or by shinnying down a rope? Is this a cave for the elite, or can a novice enter? Can I enter the Cave of Now from the tight confines of life on earth, from this place where I face my longings?

In gracious gesture, Love breathes on us. Love grabs us by the hair. Otherwise, we might never find the entrance to the Cave. Love calls us from our cramped burrow and urges us toward the cave's mouth to inhale the air of our Homeland. Jesus stands at the entrance and cries out, "I am the resurrection and the life. He who believes in me will live, even though he dies; and whoever lives and believes in me will never die. Do you believe this?" (John 11:25).

It is here that I enter the Cave of Now in a transaction between my believing soul and Jesus Christ. I enter the Cave through a network of caves, caverns as tiny and smelly as a stable-cave in Bethlehem and as cold and sterile as a borrowed tomb. I flip on my helmet light and gaze about. The darkness recedes. From the interlinking passages the angels' song, "Glory to God in the Highest," reverberates from the labyrinth past, and the proclamation, "He is Risen," gives a weeping world cause to sing.

There wasn't time for the usual burial rituals, so the body was wrapped mummy fashion and left in the cave with a tear and a prayer. The hard, fixed walls of the tomb offered no amenities, no hospitable warmth. This was a "no foolishness" place, firmly committed to meet life's eventuality, life's unwelcomed certainty: a nook of death.

In the cool and silent darkness, on the third day, life returned to that stone-walled vault. (I wonder, Does resurrection life seep back gradually or gallop in stirring dust and throwing up stones behind?)

Resurrection power so filled the cave with exuberant life that the great boulder sealing the mouth was unseated and rolled out of place. This life could not be contained. Unrestrained life, high-spirited and bursting at the seams emerged. Life came forth into a new day, seeking and saving those who long for life. The door had been forced open; no lock could withstand it, no company of centurion guards could prevent it. This same mighty power that raised Jesus from the dead and sent death reeling backwards, came as a dynamo to inhabit the fragile human shell. When Jesus took back His life in that tomb-cave, He achieved a cosmic victory and came laden with spoils, showering those who believe with Life. Life *now*.

Jesus never spoke of His death as the end of His life.

He used the image of a seed falling into the ground and dying only to bring forth more life, fuller life, greener life. His death was an "exodus." His "departure" was a journey to lead His people out of slavery into the promised land. Jesus' death and resurrection are inseparable. The Resurrection gives meaning and culmination to His death. They are a package deal inspired by longing.

The Resurrection is imperative in the scheme of what God is about. Jesus' resurrection is meant to flag me awake to another possibility, another realm of reality, another me, which is the very stuff for which I've been longing.

—

I open the door a crack only for a moment. In He floods, like the breath of a cave. He exerts the most gentle pressure. He comes with a mind of His own, unbending but thoroughly reasonable. A most gracious house guest, He moves about quietly, unobtrusively, never makes a mess; but He leaves marks of His presence everywhere.

Although He comes softly, He may as well have yanked me by the hair into another dimension, another world. I find myself in unknown territory, badly in need of an interpreter. He comes alongside, whispers in my ear, tutors me in the ways of this ancient-contemporary culture. And as in any new culture, I find myself lacking the vocabulary for heart-to-heart communication. He translates my guttural groanings into understandable language.

This Guide to a new reality comes to direct the tour and keep me from taking the wrong bus. He teaches me how to move in a crowd, how to slip in a side door and lay low for a bit, how to get a window seat and what to keep my eyes open for. And as I gaze enraptured, my substance softens, becomes more supple. In the *now* experience, He is the ever-present water that erodes, transforms, wears away rough spots, and deposits minerals to build new structures, some from the top down, others from the bottom up. I am changed. My heart flows into previously unknown recesses, pressed, shaped, stamped by the influence of Jesus Christ Himself.

The Greek word for this Love that sets up housekeeping in my soul is *paraclete*. The word *paraclete* conjures strange images in my mind of someone jumping from an airplane in armor. Instead, He descends light as a dove, a breath, and dances like flaming tongues above my head.

Paraclete means "to call beside"—a comforter, an advocate. Christ's alter ego. He is the dove of peace nesting in our hearts and the bracing steel rod who gives the brand of courage so boldly displayed by the earliest disciples. He is the mortar that keeps fractured and upheaved lives from wildly blowing apart. He's the One who plants a word in the ear and sows a thought in the mind, who prompts and prods and yells, "Heads up!"

As He enters us, we enter the Cave of Now. It is an exchange. Don Benedetto, an Italian reformer in the 1500s, describes the transaction in terms of marriage. The Groom, Christ, receives His bride's "peculiar dowry" (her sins) and she shares in His wealth. Everything becomes mutual. Christ lugs her sins to the Cross to extricate her from them and she partakes in all that is His. She becomes heir to His fortune. The transfer takes place like a ransom drop, in secret. His death for mine. His life for mine.

Ambrose likens the exchange to Jacob in the Old Testament, the second-born twin, who tricks his rather blind and infirm father into giving him the firstborn's blessing. Jacob executes the scam by disguising himself as his brother. Old sightless Isaac catches a whiff of Esau's clothes, dismisses his misgivings, and hands over the birthright. Ambrose says the believing soul must come to the Father dressed as Christ, our elder brother, to receive the blessing. The way Home depends on being mistaken for Jesus Christ. It is a glorious deception. And God is the perpetrator and victim in this divine hoax of mistaken identity. He says, "For you died, and your life is now hidden with Christ in God. When Christ, who is your life, appears, then you also will appear with him in glory" (Colossians 3:3-4).

Over the entrance to the Cave of Now hangs a blinking sign: "Now this is eternal life: that they may know you, the only true God, and Jesus Christ, whom you have sent." Eternal life begins when I step across the cavern opening. I enter the Cave and God signs the promissory note, slaps the down payment on the table, and slips the engagement ring on my finger. This is not Heaven, but the Spirit of God lives in me and I sample the first taste of what is ahead. This is precisely what my longing heart is starving for.

—

May I enter more fully into the NOW that Your longing made possible. Thank You for seizing me by the hair, for rescuing me from the jaws of my longing, for bringing me into the cave of NOW. I want to experience You as fully as I can this side of Heaven.

A new life lived on earth, indwelt by the Holy Spirit of God, a child of God mistaken for Christ Himself, eternal life begun below, NOW. I rejoice that I have had my head jerked back by Love and that I have been apprehended by Life. Thank You.

CHAPTER EIGHT

A NEW HOME FOR A NEW HEART

MAKING OUR HOME IN CHRIST

UNTIL WE'RE HOME AT LAST

Oh Lord, thou art our home,

to whom we fly,

And so hast always been,

from age to age.[1]

Francis Bacon

The Roman emperor Charlemagne lost his first three wives to early deaths, not uncommon in the ninth century. According to legend, Charlemagne determined not to remarry, but his counselors sent for the beautiful Princess Fastrada wishing to secure happiness for their emperor and an heir to the throne. Charlemagne loved Fastrada from the start, married her, and lived with her in warm affection.

The legend goes on. It was more than her beauty that compelled such devotion. Fastrada wore a magical gold ring that bound Charlemagne to love any who possessed it. When Fastrada died in an epidemic, Charlemagne could not bear to be separated from his adored queen. His bishop, concerned for Charlemagne's health and welfare, slipped Fastrada's ring on his own finger while Charlemagne slept. When Charlemagne awoke the next morning, he consented to have Fastrada buried. Now he deemed the bishop his wisest counselor and sought his company and wisdom in every matter. This became so burdensome to the bishop that one night he rode far into the forest and threw the ring into the center of a still lake. No one possessed the ring, yet in ways unknown to Charlemagne it continued to haunt him, to cause restlessness and distraction.

One day Charlemagne ventured into the woods with his huntsmen in hopes that the excitement of the hunt might clear his mind and refresh his spirit. However, the power of the ring drew him off by himself until he gazed upon that enchanted pool. Great joy overcame Charlemagne. He felt as if he had come home.

On the surface of the water, Charlemagne saw a vision: a reflection of tall, elegant towers rising in majesty, an image mirrored before him that had no earthly counterpart or origin. Charlemagne's heart stirred in love for this place. He determined to build the palace of Aix-la-Chapelle, the capitol of his realm, on the spot and in the likeness of the vision he saw on the waters.

—

When I saw a pale watercolor of Charlemagne settled, almost rooted, on the margin of the lake, staring at a reality as yet unrealized, seeing more than was there, I thought of those who live in this world but have received a glimmer of Heaven.

In the painting, yellow leaves float on the water's surface. Soon those dry and dying leaves, severed from their life, would succumb to the lake, their waterlogged forms sinking heavily to the bottom to decay, and Charlemagne's soldiers could watch it happen. But the image of the palace that trembled on the surface was only visible to Charlemagne. To others, that castle was a fairy call, a hallucination, a failure to deal with reality. But what rose up from the lake was reality, robust and eternal for Charlemagne. What Charlemagne caught sight of shimmering on the ripples he made his home.

Like Charlemagne, I catch sight of a new reality reflected on the waters. I desire to live in a dwelling based on the image I've seen. I am held on earth by a sense of obligation and natural gravitational force, but this place is no longer home. As I attend to duties here, an ivory palace glistens on the backs of my eyeballs. I know I can't return to the old address. New wine needs new wineskins. I need a home, here and now, a place between earth and Heaven, from which to face this world and to prepare for the next. Is there anywhere a suitable dwelling for this new heart?

As I yearn, an invitation arrives. A word comes to me, comes from eternity past, borne along on currents of longing. Homey and mysterious words come and hang suspended, waiting. The words are offered yesterday, today and tomorrow from a sacred yearning greater than my own: "Abide in me and I in you" (John 15:4, KJV).

What does this mean? I ask, as Mary did two thousand years ago. How can this be? Can these words be intended for me, an earthdweller, a suburban believer?

Yet strangely, this incredible proposition stirs an affirming resonance within me. My unconscious instinct is homesick for this very arrangement. I will make my home in Him.

My knees quake. Who would ever insinuate that God might be drawn into a domestic arrangement of mutual habitation? Such a thing would be an affront to Deity, except that He proposed and promoted the idea Himself. Just as He might be aghast if we were so brazen as to suggest such a thing, He may be affronted that we so casually refuse His offer. *Selah.*

The offer brings me face-to-face with the longing of God, our Maker. He roams beyond the universe, He makes the earth His footstool, He rides upon the oceans, but He chooses to make the regenerate human heart His home. He left Heaven to make His "temple in thy breast" as John Donne said. Jesus abandoned Heaven to live in me; a large price to pay for a ramshackle home.

Equally startling, He calls us to make our home *in* Him. He opens His being to us, flings wide the gates, and invites us into the holy place that we might live there forever.

The idea of living in God contains something of the mystery of the Godhead. "The Father is in me, and I in the Father," Jesus said in John 10:38. And something of the mystery of the oneness of His followers: "I have given them the glory that you gave me, that they may be one as we are one. I in them and you in me" (John 17:22-23). It is a oneness like food ingested that becomes inseparable from who we are. "Just as the living Father sent me and I live because of the Father, so the one who feeds on me will live because of me" (John 6:57).

Mysterious oneness. "On that day you will realize that I am in my Father, and you are in me, and I am in you. . . . If anyone loves me, he will obey my teaching. My Father will love him, and we will come to him and make our home with him" (John 14:20,23).

Yes is the key that opens the door into Christ, our home. He stands at the door, knocking. I say *yes* and undo the latch. Will I make my home with Him? *Yes.* If we are to make our home together, He says, I must remain with Him. Will I? *Yes.* This living arrangement is not a democracy. We will not take a vote when we disagree. He is Lord, after all. He will decide for us. *Yes*—yes upon yes, an uncrafted, voluntary stack of yeses reaching into Heaven. The walls of our life together are built by my *yeses* mortared by His grace, wisdom, and love. I must be willing to live in the white truth of His Presence. Here I build my home in God, on earth, in intimacy, in union. This is the vision reflected on the waters.

The house I grew up in was small, but was blessed with an attic and an accumulation documenting our existence. The temperature prevented long explorations, but even on a hurried expedition I searched expectantly, hoping to turn up an ancient rune or a brittle parchment, the key to treasure and adventure. Home was a safe place, a place to venture from and eagerly to return to. Home was, also, a place of adventure in itself. Home was not idyllic, but it was a structure of substance. A real location in an illusory world.

Everybody needs a home, a place to hurry to in times of joy and trouble, a haven from which to sort out life's complexities, a place of comfort and fortification. Physical homelessness is tragic. Spiritual homelessness also leaves us standing in the open, vulnerable. When severe stresses bombarded Daniel, he took shelter in his God.

Daniel lived in the world of office politics and professional jealousy. The new king of Babylon, Darius, appointed 120 satraps to rule his kingdom. Daniel so distinguished himself above his contemporaries by his exceptional qualities that the king planned to set him over the whole kingdom. The satraps looked for a way to discredit Daniel. Since Daniel's conduct, character, and work were faultless, they came to the conclusion, "We will never find any basis of charges against this man Daniel unless it has something to do with the law of his God" (Daniel 6:5).

They set up Daniel with a scheme they pushed on King Darius. For thirty days, the decree stated, no one could pray to anyone but the king. The penalty for disregarding the edict: the lion's den. Then they stamped the plan: irrevocable.

When Daniel learned that the decree was published,

"he went home." Everyone needs a home in times like that. For Daniel, it was more than beating a path to an escape hatch. Daniel went home, climbed the stairs to his upper room where the windows faced Jerusalem, and prayed three times a day as was his established practice.

As I read these verses, I see his physical home, especially those upstairs windows that faced Jerusalem as the counterpart of another Home. Daniel made a physical location within his home a sacred meeting place. In the act of hurrying into the privacy of his home, up the stairs to that upper room, Daniel illustrated the spirit of flinging open windows godward in prayer. Daniel took shelter in his God. What Daniel did in the material world reflected what was happening in his heart. Daniel knew in times of trouble to make his home in God.

As the psalmist says, "Let everyone who is godly pray to you while you may be found; surely when the mighty waters rise, they will not reach him. You are my hiding place; you will protect me from trouble and surround me with songs of deliverance" (Psalm 32:6-7).

Of course, home is more than a hiding place. Daniel hurried home, not to cry in his beer, not to take a sedative, not to lay low until thirty days had passed. For Daniel home was a place to clarify issues, nourish his faith and commitment, strengthen his resolve, and enjoy a moment of respite from the biting wind before he faced, quite literally, the lions.

Consciously or unconsciously, we place our home in the center of the map we draw. All the world, the far reaches of the universe, radiate from this place, so intimate and domestic. Wherever we may travel, regardless of how long we are gone, there is an anchor that holds secure one end of our rope. For better or worse, we never fully leave home. And when we make God Himself our dwelling place, we need *never* leave Home.

—

Emily Dickinson never went anywhere. She holed up at home for most of her life writing poetry. In a letter to a childhood friend in which she declined an invitation to visit, the reclusive poet wrote, "I thank you Abiah, but I don't go from home, unless emergency leads me by the hand, and then I do it obstinately, and draw back if I can."[2]

How did poetry come from that homebound soul, I wonder? Or maybe that is just the sort of soul from which poetic thought flows most easily. Scholars report that Walt Whitman rarely left his room. Maybe homebodies draw from founts that restless runarounds never find. Perhaps the familiar hearth dispenses an elixir for the soul, a balm that eludes nomads. Perhaps that great talent, Coleridge, wrote so few poems because he lacked a home base. Perhaps "The milk of Paradise" is cultivated only in private, in silence, in one's own closet, and until we learn to make God our dwelling place, we will wander this earth like frenzied tourists having lost sight of our final Home.

—

Oh, my heart, stay at home. Refuse your frantic bent. Settle quietly in the blessing to Benjamin: "Let the beloved of the LORD *rest secure in him, for he shields him all day long, and the one the* LORD *loves rests between his shoulders"* (Deuteronomy 33:12).

CHAPTER NINE

SATISFIED, BUT HUNGRY STILL

CHRIST IS BOTH THIRST QUENCHER

AND THIRST STIRRER

We taste Thee, O Thou Living Bread,

And long to feast upon Thee still:

We drink of Thee, the Fountainhead

And thirst our souls from Thee to fill.

Attributed to Saint Bernard of Clairvaux (1090–1153)

The woman at the well had an incredible thirst. I know that not because she was at the well at noon, when most women had long ago drawn their water and retreated to the sheltering shade of their homes. I know it because she had five husbands, and the man she currently lived with was not her husband at all. She stood at the desert well in the heat of the day leaving a wake of men behind her. Poor, parched woman! A sea of men cannot take away this burning thirst. It is glaring midday and stifling calm beneath a searing sun.

She is hot and dry. Her dragon thirst uncoils and wrenches. Thirst keeps her looking and hoping that the next man will somehow satisfy her longing. One man after another. A parade of hope . . . and disappointment. Does she yet realize her pattern? Her thirst drives her from one profane altar to another, a tottering trail from one promising mirage to the next. Her life is a series of dry wells.

Like that ancient mariner, does she sense the mocking irony, "Water, water, everywhere, and not a drop to drink"? But she can't quit the search. A thirst this demanding must be tended. Thirst keeps her alert to possibilities; hope keeps her from despair.

Then she meets a man at Jacob's well. Will she be disappointed again? He's hard to understand, this man. The conversation is about everyday things like water and thirst, or is it? He puts a funny twist on everything. He is a stranger, but He knows about the men in her past. *Knowing.* Yes, that's the word she'd use to describe Him. Not just knowing about her personal life, but about secret things that touch the spirit.

Everything that happens at the well that day has to

do with those deep, hidden yearnings of the spirit, with thirst and satisfaction. He tells her she can ask for and receive living water and never thirst again. He says that if she drinks the water He gives, it will become in her a spring of water welling up to eternal life. Is He just another con man, promising but not delivering? She is, after all, a vulnerable woman, susceptible to promises. The end of the story isn't recorded, but I suspect, if her experience is anything like mine, that she found in that Water what she was aching for.

Like the woman at the well, I had a heart all aflame with yearning. As far back as I can remember, at the core of my being, a throbbing desire pulsed its little song. The song was sweetly sorrowful and, evidently, very hungry. I never heard the words, but I think the tune said, "Feed me" and "I thirst." It taxed my creativity to find some morsel to feed it, to blunt the hunger, to mute the cry. I threw everything I could think of to its insatiable gut.

Sometimes the chant would subside; sometimes it would rant, driving me to make some unholy offering to it. That song kept me off balance and restless, kept me from curling up comfortably in this world when I was made for another. My thirst song prepared me to receive the water of life, to accept the gift of God.

When you think of it, thirsts and hungers are gifts in themselves. Preliminary gifts. Gifts, like compasses and maps, intended to help us to our destination. Gifts, like John the Baptist, that come to prepare the way. God gives the gift of thirst and invites us to satisfy our thirst in Him. He is the Spring in search of thirsty people. The Spring extends the invitation, "Come! Whoever is thirsty, let him come; and whoever wishes, let him take the free gift of the water of life" (Revelation 22:17). He continually bubbles forth like an offering within cup-dipping range.

When my thirst confronted the Water that was offered, I faced a high noon showdown. I sensed that either this Water would satisfy where all others had failed, or else I would do my stint on earth plagued with the gnawing.

When I first came to Jesus I was thirsty as ever. I wanted the water He offered. I believed; I drank. A spring sluiced up inside me just as He said. It was for this water I thirsted my whole life. The Living Water permeated the immense longing of my youth. Thirty-some years later, whatever the changing shape of my longings, He alone still satisfies.

I can't describe my experience with Christ any more than the woman at the well could describe hers. All she could tell her friends was that "He told me everything I ever did." Like falling in love, its very nature prevents analysis. As a girl, totally undaunted, I used to ask, "How will I know if I'm in love?" The answer I received most often was, "You'll know."

You ask, "How do you know that Jesus is what you were thirsting for, that all along the yearning was to bring you into some vital connection with Him? How do you know that the homesickness embedded at your core existed because you were meant to live with Him for ever and ever?"

I answer, "I know."

Newly believing, satisfied, and thoroughly ignorant, I was drawn to read that enigmatic book, the Bible. The fog began to lift off the pages. The sun drove glistening motes through the haze. I met God on every page. I was still new and ignorant, but the Water of Life began to hydrate my dry soul.

When E. Stanley Jones was new and ignorant, he would press his lips to truths that moved him as he read his New Testament. His kiss expresses the very emotion I felt.

Reading this book was one astonishment after another. I was startled by the injunction to watch for His coming. Unlearned though I was, I determined to watch. At night I sat long at my bedroom window like a watchman on the city wall. Constellations rotated. The night wore on and I retreated to bed with every intention of sleep. I lay there overcome with the desire to sit and watch. I returned to the window with a shivering anticipation. I'm not sure what I thought might happen, but I was satisfied and hungry for more of Him.

Like the window, the Japanese cherry tree in my parents' yard became a trysting place. Filled with Living Water, I stood beneath the branches. Sometimes I spoke or sang. More often I just drank the water offered. I lingered under the cherry tree, conscious of the demands of this world and I experienced something of my Homeland. The material world made demands on me; it was time for class or dinner. Time to open a book and take notes or converse at the table, but images of Home threw their shadows on the walls of my mind and I felt the tug. Like the force exerted by the conjunction of two neighboring planets, my Homeland exerted its gravitational force. At the first opportunity I hurried back to the window or the cherry tree.

At the window and the cherry tree, I faced an unexpected juxtaposition: I was brimful yet hungry for more of Him. He quenched my thirst at the same time He stoked my desire. Nothing about this paradox seemed amiss. I was simply satisfied and happily ravenous.

And I am not alone in this experience.

Evidently, Moses couldn't get enough of God either. God talked with him from a burning bush and descended in a pillar of cloud when Moses entered the tent of meeting to pray. It was an extraordinary relationship. God said they talked "face-to-face" like friends. But Moses wanted more. He wanted God's presence and a fuller revelation of God's glory. The wonder found in personal connection with God didn't extinguish his longings; it satisfied and ignited them.

Isaiah saw the Lord enthroned and exalted, and the encounter undid him. He trembled in awe. The brush with brilliance was almost more than he could bear. But he wanted more. "My soul yearns for you in the night; in the morning my spirit longs for you" (Isaiah 26:9).

Like Isaiah, the more Julian of Norwich knew of God, the more she longed to know. "I saw Him, and sought Him; and I had Him, I wanted Him," she said.[1] William of Saint Thierry expressed it this way: "Is the soul that so thirsts for God as for the fount of life ever so satisfied that it cries, 'Enough'?"[2]

Like a spirit awakened from a deadening sleep, I set out on the Homeward journey. The landscape is strange and inviting. The terrain awash in secret meeting places: a bedroom window, a cherry tree, a private corner of the window seat behind the drapes, a forest inlet carpeted with pine needles, a sunny spot against a rock, an overstuffed chair with footstool. From every quarter, the call comes. His voice and my own longings lure me to set up little temporary homes. Inside and out, domestic and wild, grand vistas and intimate corners become personal sanctuaries, places to pause and saturate the peculiar contour of my longing space.

—

Satisfied and hungry still. This jarring paradox is the bridge that spans the expanse between here and eternity . . . and Home. It is the cable among the intricate tangle of webs defining life on earth. This is the rope strung from the house to the barn to get us safely through the blizzard. It is both a paradox and model for the Homeward-bound heart.

The paradox is a mystery that's easy to live with, one I feel no need to question. Everything about my continued desire seems integral to this relationship. Perhaps the only true confidence we have that we've made connection with Him is that He fills our hollow place and stirs our desire to drink again.

To the satisfied and still hungry soul, He says, Eat. Drink. Meeting places became feeding places and watering holes. There is no boredom in Christ, no sodden satiety. He is thirst quencher and thirst stirrer. Peter Damian said, "Always eager and always satisfied, the elect have what they desire: satiety never becomes wearisome, and hunger, kept alive by desire, never becomes painful. Desiring, they eat constantly, and eating, they never cease to desire."[3]

—

Lord, the sweetest, most painful thing in my life is the longing, the hunger and thirst for more of You. Thank You for stirring my need and desire. Call me again to the window.

CHAPTER TEN

PLOW HORSES AND FLEDGLING FINCHES

OUR LONGINGS KEEP US

FROM LOSING SIGHT

—

How lovely is your dwelling place,

O LORD Almighty!

My soul yearns, even faints, for the courts of

the LORD;

my heart and my flesh cry out

for the living God.

Even the sparrow has found a home,

and the swallow a nest for herself,

where she may have her young—a place

near your altar,

O LORD Almighty, my King and my God.

Blessed are those who dwell in your house;

they are ever praising you.

Blessed are those whose strength is in you,

who have set their hearts on pilgrimage.

Psalm 84:1-5

—

A house finch built her nest in the wreath on our front door. The tiny hair-lined nest embraces four gray-green eggs. I consider it a mixed blessing. Once swallows chose to grace our porch supports with their mud-caked home. I taped newspaper to the porch floor under their nest to catch the consequences of their presence. Guests always asked about the newspaper. I told them I was paper-training the birds. Despite the mess, I liked watching the hatchlings all mouths agape and the parents busy flitting about so unselfishly to feed their insatiable and unappreciative young.

I look through the glass in our door and meet mother finch's bright eye or scrutinize the eggs for first signs of life. I have a strange sense of intimacy as I watch this bird's small body rise and fall with each breath on the other side of partially frosted glass. Does she recognize my face as human, as something to be feared? She is alert but stays put. When I enter the porch to water the geraniums, she usually flies to the top of the neighbor's tree. A picnic bench blocks access to the porch and sports a hand-lettered sign: Do not enter porch—bird nesting.

How does a bird decide where to build a nest, this nest so homey and serene? What criteria does instinct favor? I can't imagine that a blue door with a window in it and a vine wreath decorated with eucalyptus and white paper ribbon would fit the bill. What drew her to our porch, our door, our wreath?

The singer of the ancient Jewish song, evidently, has some sort of nesting instinct himself. He envies birds nesting near the altar in the tabernacle. It seems no matter where he is, his heart keeps winging back to the presence of God. He yearns for a constant, complete experience of

God, but that cannot be—not yet. This desire shapes his values and thinking. He would rather be a doorkeeper in God's tent than share the lifestyles of the rich and famous. Oh, to praise God without interruption, without thought of reaping, sowing, or storing away in barns; without the circumstances that create distance between himself and God's house.

This man is a pilgrim in the purest sense of the word. He is in a perpetual state of yearning, never fully free of desire for that Place and Presence. He thinks about his *last* trip to that tent of meeting or his *next* trip there. Sometimes only memory and hope keep him going. The lyrics of his song climb and dive like a bird in flight: He sings: "My soul yearns, even faints, for the courts of the Lord; my heart and my flesh cry out for the living God."

What attracts the singer to this tent of worship? What current moves just beneath the surface urging him toward God? Why will this man spend much of his life on earth in longing? Could Donald Bloesch be right? He says, "Our greatest affliction is not anxiety or even guilt but rather homesickness—a nostalgia or ineradicable yearning to be at home with God."[1]

I'm a pilgrim, too, of sorts, a homesick wanderer who yearns to nest in the bosom of God, undisturbed and undistracted. I yearn because on earth I face distraction within as well as without. Although every glimmer of Heaven perceived starts some small fire in me, I am, unfortunately, almost always a person of little fires. This world oppressively snuffs out patches of infant heat before they get half a start. The faint smell of smoke reaches me, but I have already turned to something else. Sometimes the scent is more of an irritation than a reminder, because I cannot remember its source.

—

Two months out of Egypt, and a nation of recently freed slaves is already winding their way back to bondage in their minds. Behind them the neon glow of Egypt lights up the night. They remember with relish the garlic and leeks they ate there. Just as the woman at the well mistakenly hopes that someone tall, dark, and handsome will fill her emptiness, these ex-slaves think the answer might be in the garlic and leek hot-plate special.

Perhaps we all fix our eyes on things that can never satisfy our hunger. The land promised to us gets lost in the pressures of feeding our faces and keeping the wolf away from the door. We have a way of adjusting to slavery, of preferring the certainty of lunch over Heaven.

Moses leads this nation of freed and griping slaves in circles in the desert. It isn't an easy job. They have zigzagging hearts and stiff necks. They are desperate for a need they can't walk around, so God turns up the heat. God sends them an attention grabber: *hunger*. Hunger is bold. It intrudes to center stage and hogs the limelight. Hunger can't be ignored. In kindness God afflicts a nation unaccustomed to freedom with hunger. Without it, they might wander in circles forever, or wind their way back to the land of their enslavement. Without hunger they might neglect that which is essential to life.

Then, just as Living Water came courting a love-starved woman, Bread from Heaven throws a daily picnic in a barren waste somewhere between Egypt and Canaan and rains down manna. God knows pilgrims require bread from Heaven. A soul cannot live on earthly bread alone. Spiritual nourishment, as refreshing as dew itself, is essential for the desert trek between captivity and the promised land.

I long, but my longings are different from the stirrings I felt when I was homesick with no idea of what I was homesick for. Then, I seldom recognized the longings for what they were. Thirty-some years into the journey, the longings come as a known companion. I know the Voice. I remember why I hunger and what will satisfy. Longings do not come to a vacuum, but to that point of my finding and believing, to that vital connection under the fig tree. A holy homesickness accompanies my soul on its journey from the pear tree to the fig tree of Augustine's search to the cherry tree in my parents' yard and, finally, to the tree of life in my Homeland.

Sometime I still misread my longings and meander dead-end trails. Sometimes when the Lord comes calling, when He pauses just outside my window, when He peers in through the lattice and beckons me to enjoy the garden with Him, I hang back. I have my reasons. I'm already in bed, my feet are washed. The call comes, but I refuse the invitation. I choose the comfort of a warm bed rather than pad across the cold floor and meet Him. But the bed is no longer warm and comfortable. My longings see to that. I'm restless, lonely for His company. I regret my reticence. I get up and seek Him on the path that heads Home where, when time is over, we will spend eternity together.

Longings keep my soul from drying up; they court me to keep me from losing sight of the land of my dreams. I tend to stray. My desire for Home is always at risk and in need of nurturing.

Today when yearnings summon, I respond. I let longings lead me into the garden. This is not that garden of delight God planted for Adam, where God visited His creation. Man was driven from that garden and may not return to it. The garden I enter is not a perfect place. These surrogate gardens, where I stand under the cherry tree, remind me that I am an alien on a planet that is not my home. My estrangement unnerves at the same time it comforts me. I don't like being a stranger in the only home I've ever known, but the sense of really belonging somewhere else cheers me. The thought cheered G. K. Chesterton, too. He writes, "We have come to the wrong star . . . that is what makes life at once so splendid and so strange. The true happiness is that we don't fit. We come from somewhere else. We have lost our way."[2]

Like you, I have a life on earth, but I can't let it get in the way of heavensent yearnings. I must take the path through the garden.

———

I have a poor little cottage garden, mostly perennials, that struggles admirably beneath the withering Colorado sun and wind. The growing season is short (we can have snow in May and September), but once the garden gets going, it shows no modesty or restraint. Color spills over, fragrance mounts on fragrance, and lumbering bumble bees, like airborne tanks, rumble over the sweet centers of every bloom.

But blooms don't come easily. Where I live, the soil needs constant amending. If I didn't care about the flowers, I wouldn't give much thought to the dirt in my backyard. But I'm alert to the soil and read that an agriculture department scientist said the mysteries of outer space are no more perplexing than those found in the rhizosphere, the root zone of plants. He described that world as teeming with minerals, gases, water, insects, earthworms, microscopic nematode worms, microorganisms, living and dead plant roots, and the chemicals they emit.

The soil of my life is complex, too, and needs amending. My life gets hard, compacted, like a well-trod path. Soil lies in shallow piles among the rocks. Weeds prosper. Thorny, coarse, and spiny plants spring up, wild and strangling. Climate, pests, and disease hinder the tender sprout of new life. This world leeches the soil of my soul.

Into this nutrient-poor soil my life in Christ is planted. Care and attention is needed if it is to flourish. The Gardener of the soul says, "I, the LORD, watch over it; I water it continually. I guard it day and night so that no one may harm it" (Isaiah 27:3). Then He sends a dose of homesickness to engage us in the process. Every soul that is truly alive is watered with longings.

Our longings, those workhorses, those servants of God, faithful and incessant, come for a purpose. They buck and heave, whinny and snort, as they harrow our hearts. They endow and enlarge the soul to desire and receive God. Their muscles bunch and strain as they keep us moving toward Home. Longings with big feet and a noble vocation stir up fluttering birds to seek a homey spot to set up housekeeping. Like birds in spring, the believing heart has a nesting instinct inspired by longing.

These longings keep a sharp edge to our lives, keep them from a flaccid shapelessness that is comfortable but damned. This work God does in us makes us sensitive to His presence so that we can enjoy it when it is given or feel the void when it is withdrawn. A healthy soul pines for something beyond this world. It is the pain and pleasure of seeking God that causes the soul to thrive. The ache for Home is a mercy, our unease absolutely necessary. Homesickness is a kind reminder, faithful to the end, that without guarding, even a pilgrim might set up permanent camp here beside dry wells and drink from broken cisterns.

—

The birds were just two weeks old, and then they were no more. One morning we found the nest sprawled facedown on the porch, either blown down or pulled down by a cat. We searched but found no trace of the four fledglings. Did they ever get to test their wings? Or like athletes pulled up lame minutes before the race, or virgins struck down before the wedding night, did they come up short?

I swept away their droppings, but I can't bring myself quite yet to wash the last signs of their life from the door, to wash away all that remains as a testament to their ever having lived. It is my way of saying to their parents that I am sorry, that I know they lived, that I think they were beautiful and promising, that I have known sorrow, too, and that I am grateful they chose to grace our door with their fragile, pulsing life.

We looked for them, but like Elijah, some heavenly chariot must have spirited them off. They are gone. Raptured. All that remains is encrusted to our door. It reminds me that a home on a blue door is brief and hazardous. Even my uneasy questions stir my longing to be where winds and cats can't destroy.

I hold the fallen nest and reflect. Neither will I go on here forever. One day all that is left of me can be swept away or saved as a token remembrance by those who care enough to hold me in their minds for a while longer. Life on earth is short, but a better country lies ahead. Until I can be near God in the intimacy and perfection of that land, I gratefully accept the company of longings.

—

Longings, work your work in me. Flash a clearer, more enduring picture of Heaven on my heart. My vision of eternal reality too quickly fades, bleached almost invisible by this world's light. Use whatever means, whatever strategy, to induce my soul to draw near God. Come as lurching plow horses or fledgling finches. Keep me moving. Point me Home.

HOME
AT LAST

CHAPTER ELEVEN

WORTH DYING FOR

ALL CREATION GROANS FOR RELEASE

—

When dawns the Invisible;

the Unseen its truth reveals;

My outward sense is gone,

my inward essence feels;

Its wings are almost free—

its home, its harbour found;

Measuring the gulf, it stoops,

and dares the final bound.[1]

Emily Brontë

—

One year we camped in the Okanogan Valley that runs from eastern Washington into Canada. Money was short; we borrowed a two-man tent and set out for the hot, dry heat of summer. The gray days and weak sun of Seattle, where we lived, had gotten to me. This trip was my husband's creative solution for a family vacation.

Despite everything we read in the brochures, the sun did not shine on us. The days were cold and disappointing. I wore all the clothes I brought every day, and nights were no respite. I felt panicky under the claustrophobic slant of the tent and fearful bears might eat me if I slept outside. On our last night in the tent, torrential rains attacked and won.

That tent was better than nothing, but by scant margin in my opinion. I was out of sight of the bears, but not out of reach. I was out of the full force of the rain, but not kept dry. The tent allowed me to sleep out of doors, but encased me in a suffocating cocoon. I was consoled that the tent was a temporary dwelling. I knew I had something better awaiting me at home. My husband said my brightest smile of the trip came at his suggestion that we cut our vacation short and head home. I was a girl again in full anticipation of a safe, dry place with the ceiling eight feet above my head. Yet strangely, I felt a certain fondness for that tent.

I feel a far deeper attachment to the tent that is me, my flesh and bones—that part of me that allows me to see something in the mirror. I know I'd still be me if I were burned beyond recognition, but I have trouble thinking of myself apart from this container.

My physical body houses my inner self, keeps the rain off my soul, and lets me squint at the sun. My clothing keeps me private and somewhat protected. But flesh and fabric can't keep out a howling wind or a driving sleet, so I seek shelter in a two-story house on a cul-de-sac. I like the house, but even if I lived in a castle, I'd feel the draft. This is not my place.

Paul writes, "We groan, longing to be clothed with our heavenly dwelling" (2 Corinthians 5:2). Paul, of course, was too bright to mix his metaphors in ignorance. He intentionally links the image of a fisherman's linen blouse with our dwelling in Heaven. We groan for Home, for a true fit, for a seamless reality.

Paul says we groan. Maybe he is right. I think I hear the whole world groaning. Or is it only my own moan . . . or yours that I hear?

I sit hugging myself in the sunlight. I feel substantial and durable. My flesh is soft and warm and I can discern muscle and bone—my strength. I notice six small brown age marks on my left hand. Some people grimly call them grave spots. The backs of my hands have lost their youthful fleshiness. Veins and bones fan over the surface. Everywhere I look, I'm fading, wasting, failing, drooping, freckling—dying. This body is a groaning thing, the victim of time's untiring wear. The groan comes from a soul apprehensive about sleeping in the open without a tent.

When a tent is taken down, pegs are loosened and uprooted one by one. The tent flutters, sways, and lists before collapsing with billow, thud, and stirring of dust. One moment a harboring shelter, the next a limp form waiting to be folded and hauled away.

Years ago, I saw a man die in my rear-view mirror. I glanced up, watched him wrench, body, car and all, to the right, off the road, through a split rail fence into a pasture with grazing cows and horses. Stroke or heart attack, I suspect. A sudden, violent death in a tranquil pastoral scene. Unexpected, but inevitable.

Bud Ponten died last week. Several people thought they were in the wrong room when they saw him laid out in the funeral home. Bud had cerebral palsy that cranked and twisted his body to uncomfortable angles. Now Bud measured six feet six inches all stretched out. Released. Gone the neck brace. Gone the pain. Gone the contorted gait. Gone the longing. The groaning ceased.

For me the groan continues. I'm a camper far from home stuck in an inadequate tent facing the storm. This tent that is my body lets in a draft. This body that I've chummed around with since birth, that grew up with me, that sports the nicks and dings of my living, doesn't fit quite right.

I groan with anticipation. I lean forward teetering on the edge of my chair. I balance precariously on a fine thread, hanging on to my tent with one hand and reaching shakily toward an invisible hope, a promised Home.

The groan isn't to be released from a wheelchair or a bad marriage. The groan comes from the desire for completion, for culmination, for consummation. I'm weary and disgusted with being stifled in my humanity. I want to be set free from the vise that compresses me to a fraction of my intended height, that keeps me from reaching my full stature, that forces me to stumble and shuffle through life when I was meant to leap and bound. But most of all, I desire a newness that will allow me to enter fully into the Relationship I've begun on earth, to fully claim my family inheritance.

I long for full redemption, and I don't groan alone. All that exists in the created world is bound together by a moan. "We know that the whole creation has been groaning as in the pains of childbirth right up to the present time. Not only so, but we ourselves, who have the firstfruits of the Spirit, groan inwardly as we wait eagerly for our adoption as sons, the redemption of our bodies" (Romans 8:22-23). The groan shudders through creation to a civilization self-destructing. Even the angels lean forward in anticipation waiting for God to bring to completion the purpose of the ages; in that day, grace will become glory, promise will become tangible, faith will become sight, hope will become experience. In that day God's good intentions will be fully displayed.

Redemption is the great theme of the Bible, and homesickness seeps from the pores of every page. Redemption is a process with a climax, a longing with a consummation, a divine romance that proceeds to marriage.

Jesus left home, like Abraham's servant, to seek a bride and take her home with Him. He came to earth to court her, to pay the bride price, then return home to prepare a place for her. He longs for her to be with Him, to see His glory, the glory given Him before the creation of the world (John 17:24).

Jesus, in longing, utters the traditional lines from the engagement ceremony, "In my Father's house are many rooms; if it were not so, I would have told you. I am going there to prepare a place for you. And if I go and prepare a place for you, I will come back and take you to be with me that you also may be where I am" (John 14:2-3).

God prepares a place for me, a space meant for me. My needs are provided for. No need to pack the casket with rice, wine, wives, and blowgun.

The language is homey and intimate; the images are of house and rooms. Our longing was always for a sure space within a father's house, a sure place within a family, a sure reception into a loving embrace.

I pause and ponder. What kind of longing sends a creator God to fluff the pillows and turn back the sheets? I suppose the same kind of longing that propels a man to die to redeem another or the kind of longing that sends His servants out to compel the poor, crippled, blind, and lame to come in, "so that my house will be full" (Luke 14:23).

I understand my longing only as I understand something of His. My longings on earth are wild, sweet fragments of His wilder, sweeter longings. Now I see only in part, but I do see. I feed on the foreshadowing: "You will fill me with joy in your presence, with eternal pleasures at your right hand" (Psalm 16:11).

God gives us a peek into eternity when He tells us, "They are before the throne of God and serve him day and night in his temple; and he who sits on the throne will spread his tent over them. Never again will they hunger; never again will they thirst. The sun will not beat upon them, nor any scorching heat. For the Lamb at the center of the throne will be their shepherd; he will lead them to springs of living water. And God will wipe every tear from their eyes" (Revelation 7:15,17).

"Your dead will live; their bodies will rise. You who dwell in the dust, wake up and shout for joy" (Isaiah 26:19).

"He will wipe every tear from their eyes. There will be no more death or mourning or crying or pain, for the old order of things has passed away" (Revelation 21:4).

In that day I will leap like John the Baptist leapt in the womb. Exultant, joyous, astonished at myself, perfectly whole standing in like company before the living God. I will be at home in my heavenly dwelling, wearing the garment bought by Another. I stand radiant, grinning like a bride decked out on her wedding day.

My new body is like the resurrection body of Jesus Christ, for apart from the resurrection there is no hope. If life on earth is *it*, my longing is left dangling. Christ's death and resurrection are the basis and type of my hope. His death and resurrection defang death. From Christ's death and resurrection I gather courage. No . . . more, desire to exchange my dusty and tender self for a new and shining body.

As the body winds down, breaks down, opens in itself yawning holes, the groan comes whistling through, piercing the dilapidation. My body groans for what my heart and soul have groaned for all along and readies me to move Homeward. I have not cultivated the groan; the groan has cultivated me. The scaffolding of flesh and bones gives way and eternal realities stand vivid in the sunlight.

The day will come; our tent will collapse. We will wrench body, soul, and spirit off the road, through the rail fence; we will run and leap, clap our hands in unison with the applauding trees, and rush through the gates into our city. Our voices will rise in singing and praise and laughter at seeing Him exalted and all the rest of us, a motley crew on earth, in new bodies all spiffed up, scrubbed rosy clean from the inside out with glory, overcome with gratitude. We will weep and laugh and pinch ourselves at our good fortune at getting what we didn't deserve and not getting what we did deserve.

Jesus calls in that day, "Come, you who are blessed by my Father; take your inheritance, the kingdom prepared for you since the creation of the world" (Matthew 25:34).

No more leaky tent;
No fear of bears.
The ceiling is high and clear above my head.
My place; my space.
My own bed.
Warm and dry.

Safe and satisfied.
No tears.
No pain.
The groan has ceased.

I see Him, whom my soul loves.
The vise is released.
I am released.
I am like Him, with Him,
Forever.

He leaves His tent;
The Sun of love comes for me.
His banner over me is love.
I taste the honey;
I am embraced as by the bridegroom.

I am Home.
I am free;
I am full.
I leap and dance.
I exalt in Him who my soul loves.

Come! Whoever is thirsty,
let him come;

and whoever wishes,
let him take the free gift of the water of life.

Come and see.
Come.
He is beautiful.
He is endless.
I am His and He is mine.
Forever.

Longing, no more.
Home, at last.

NOTES

Chapter One: The Homesick Heart

1. Frederick Buechner, *The Magnificent Defeat* (New York: Seabury Press, 1966), page 1.
2. Peter Matthiessen, *The Snow Leopard* (New York: The Viking Press, 1978), page 39.
3. Hermann Hesse, *Steppenwolf* (New York: Holt, Rinehart and Winston, 1963), page 32.
4. Frederick Buechner, *Peculiar Treasures* (San Francisco: Harper and Row, 1979), page 35.
5. C. S. Lewis, *The Pilgrim's Regress* (New York: Bantam Books, Grand Rapids: Eerdmans, 1981), page 127.
6. C. S. Lewis, *Till We Have Faces* (Grand Rapids, MI: Eerdmans, 1956), pages 74-76.
7. Graham Greene, *Graham Greene: Collected Short Stories, The Hint of an Explanation* (Middlesex, England: Penguin Books, 1986), page 33.
8. Marjorie Kinnan Rawlings, *The Yearling* (New York: Charles Scribner's Sons, Macmillan, 1967), page 14.
9. Annie Dillard, *An American Childhood* (New York: Harper & Row, 1987), pages 171-172.

Chapter Two: God Longs Too

1. Francis Thompson, *The Hound of Heaven* (New York:

Dodd, Mead and Co., 1965), page 45.
2. Athanasius, *The Incarnation of the Word of God* (New York: Macmillan, 1946), page 96.
3. James Ramsey Ullman, *The Day on Fire* (Cleveland, OH: The World Publishing Company, 1959), pages 25-26.

Chapter Three: A Word of Longing

1. Malcolm Muggeridge, as quoted in *People with a Message*, a Campus Crusade for Christ publication (1982).
2. Camera Laye, *Radiance of the King* (New York: Vintage, 1989), page 18.

Chapter Four: A Toast to Longing

1. Romano Guardini, *The Lord* (Chicago, Henry Regnery, 1954), page 398.

Chapter Five: The Tragedy of Almost

1. "The Darkling Thrush," *The Complete Poems of Thomas Hardy*, James Gibson, ed. (New York: Macmillan, 1976), page 150.
2. Kenneth Grahame, *The Wind in the Willows* (New York: Holt, Rinehart and Winston, 1980), page 67.
3. Peter Mathiessen, *The Snow Leopard* (New York: The Viking Press, 1978), page 39.
4. Blaise Pascal, *Pensées* (Middlesex, England: Penguin Books, 1966, A. J. Krailsheimer), page 101.

Chapter Six: When Longings Connect

1. Isak Dinesen, *Babette's Feast and Other Anecdotes of Destiny, The Diver* (New York: Random House, 1986), page 53.

2. Annie Dillard, *Pilgrim at Tinker Creek* (New York: Harper and Row, 1974), page 72.

3. Augustine, *Augustine: Confessions and Enchiridion* (Philadelphia: Westminster Press, 1955), page 169.

4. Augustine, page 164.

5. Augustine, page 170.

Chapter Seven: The Cave of Now

1. Chaim Potok, *The Gift of Asher Lev* (New York: Alfred A. Knopf, 1990), page 102.

2. Elizabeth Barrett Browning, "Sonnets from the Portuguese," *The Le Gallienne Book of English and American Poetry* (Garden City, NY: Garden City Publishing Co., 1935), page 286.

Chapter Eight: A New Home for a New Heart

1. Francis Bacon, as quoted by C. H. Spurgeon, *The Treasury of David*, vol. 2, part 2 (McLean, VA: MacDonald Publishing, n.d.), page 69.

2. Emily Dickinson, quoted from "Letter to a Childhood Friend," *Victoria*, vol. 3, no. 1, February 1989.

Chapter Nine: Satisfied, But Hungry Still

1. Julian of Norwich, *Selections from Revelations of Divine Love* (Nashville, TN: The Upper Room, 1963), page 15.

2. William of St. Thierry, an essay included in *The Love of God* by Bernard of Clairvaux (Portland, OR: Multnomah, 1983), page 114.

3. Peter Damian, *Late Medieval Mysticism*, vol. 13, Ray C. Petry, ed. (Philadelphia, PA: The Westminster Press, 1962), page 74.

Chapter Ten: Plow Horses and Fledgling Finches

1. Donald Bloesch, *Theological Notebook* (Colorado Springs, CO: Helmers and Howard, 1989), page 183.
2. G. K. Chesterton, *The Everlasting Man* (Garden City, NY: Doubleday Books, 1955), page 187.

Chapter Eleven: Worth Dying For

1. Emily Brontë, "The Prisoner," *The Le Gallienne Book of English and American Poetry* (Garden City, NY: Garden City Publishing Co., 1935), page 336.

AUTHOR

Jean Fleming and her husband, Roger, live in Colorado Springs, Colorado. They have three grown children. Roger and Jean are on staff with The Navigators and have served in California, Korea, Okinawa, Arizona, and Washington.

Jean is also the author of *A Mother's Heart* (NavPress, 1982) and *Finding Focus in a Whirlwind World* (Roper Press, 1991). In addition to her writing ministry, Jean speaks to women's groups.